FRANCIS HOLLAND SCHOOL

CAREERS

D1321503

how2become

Airline Pilot

Lee Woolaston

Francis Holland School NW1 6XR

WITHDRAWN

T0487

Orders: Please contact How2become Ltd, Suite 2, 50 Churchill Square Business Centre, Kings Hill, Kent ME19 4YU.

You can also order via the e mail address info@how2become.co.uk.

ISBN: 9781907558962

First published 2012

Copyright © 2012 How2become Ltd.

All rights reserved. Apart from any permitted use under UK copyright law, no part of this publication may be reproduced or transmitted in any form or by any means, electronic or mechanical, including photocopying, recording, or any information, storage or retrieval system, without permission in writing from the publisher or under licence from the Copyright Licensing Agency Limited. Further details of such licenses (for reprographic reproduction) may be obtained from the Copyright Licensing Agency Ltd, Saffron House, 6-10 Kirby Street, London EC1N 8TS.

Typeset for How2become Ltd by Molly Hill, Canada.

Printed in Great Britain for How2become Ltd by Bell & Bain Ltd, 303 Burnfield Road, Thornliebank, Glasgow G46 7UQ.

CONTENTS

DISCLAIMER

The author would like to state that he has made every effort to furnish the reader with his own opinion of the very best information available, with regards to training and becoming an Airline Pilot in the UK and in Europe. Neither the author nor the publisher will be held responsible for any subsequent failure of flight exams or flight tests, or any financial losses accrued by the reader. As illustrated in the manual, there is a potential for high financial loss and there are no guarantees of success in the licencing exams nor, indeed, securing a position as an Airline Pilot.

 how2become

INTRODUCTION

I'd like to start by saying, thank you very much for purchasing this guide. It's my intention for you to be very well informed and to get a really good head start if you decide that a career as an Airline Pilot is for you!

I'd like to briefly introduce myself and give you a glimpse of my career so far in Aviation. I am currently a Captain with a Major UK Regional Airline. I fly the Embraer 135/145 at present — a modern regional passenger jet airliner. I have approaching 5000 flying hours total time (3500 with the Airlines) and I hold a JAA ATPL. My interest in learning to fly started when I did a series of parachute jumps for cancer research. After answering lots of my questions, the pilots at the parachute club said that it would be a good idea if I stopped "bugging" them and book myself in for a trial-flying lesson. That is exactly what I did, and the rest is history! I was hooked and instinctively knew that this is what I wanted to do for a living. It's interesting that every pilot I've ever asked the question "how did you get in to flying?" Always has a unique story to tell.

I became a flying instructor ten years ago (at the time of writing) and eight years ago got my first job as an Airline Pilot. Within eighteen months I had progressed to a major regional UK Airline where I have spent the last six and a half years. I achieved my Command eighteen months ago and I have really enjoyed my career so far.

It has been my intention to write this manual for a few years to help inform people about: financing, qualifying, becoming and working as an Airline Pilot in today's market. The main reason being that there are many pitfalls along the way, which year after year lots of people become victims of, especially nowadays.

The manual is aimed at people wishing to become an Airline Pilot in Europe and specifically aimed at training, primarily, in the UK. It refers to the licensing procedures in Europe. The USA has a different licensing system, as do other countries outside of Europe.

I do not deal with conversion from non European to European licensing and vice versa in this manual. For full details of how to convert different ICAO Licenses It would be worth contacting the relevant licensing Authorities.

CHAPTER ONE
MY OBJECTIVE

Firstly, I'd like to offer you congratulations on being smart enough to purchase this manual. There was, absolutely, NOTHING like it before I set out to become an Airline Pilot. It WILL save you a lot of confusion, a lot of money, and a lot of time FACT!

My objective is to give you all of the information you need with regard to the following aspects.

What it is ACTUALLY like being an Airline Pilot and NOT how, almost everyone without exception, IMAGINES it will be like!

Although many pilots think it's one of the greatest jobs in the world, there are also some who wished they had done something else instead! I'm not intending to put people off, quite the opposite; however, I think it's best that you know the facts before spending lots of time and money, don't you?

You will learn the most efficient method for obtaining your necessary qualifications from Zero experience.

 how2become

Contrary to popular belief, you do not need ANY formal qualifications (Although of course it helps if you do have some) apart from the Aviation qualifications I will recommend you to get to become an Airline Pilot.

Other than my aviation qualifications, I have a few GCSE's, which are completely irrelevant, and qualifications from my previous career, again completely irrelevant to aviation. I know many Pilots with NO other qualifications.

Another myth is that people think that you have to be highly intelligent. I would say a good degree of common sense and a reasonable level of intelligence is more like what is required.

Regional accents are fine too, gone are the days of snobbery and jobs for the boys! That said I don't think the phrase "I got me ATPL innit" would go down too well at an interview somehow! I'm sure you know what I am trying to say!

Ladies you're all welcome too! There are lots more ladies coming into the profession these days which is good to see.

It's vital that you have a clear-cut plan of your journey through your training. I will show you how to organize this simply and effectively.

I will show you all of the pitfalls – I could have, and probably would have, lost a lot of money without this information alone, MANY people have lost MANY Thousands of pounds because of this- but you WILL NOT!

I will show you how to put together your CV so that it gets kept, and not put straight in the bin!

You will learn strategies that WILL get you interviews! In my opinion getting the interview is one of the hardest steps to becoming a pilot, I'll show you how to do it!

You will learn how to DO an Airline Interview! Many people fall down here after all the hard work of getting the interview!

I will be showing you, essential books and equipment you'll need to buy, contacts and links to websites that will help you with everything from your training *(I will give you tips on how to find the best Training Establishments to suit your needs)* to Airline Contacts, which Airlines are recruiting, Industry information, Unions, blogs and much more.

As you probably know by now it is very expensive to train to become an Airline Pilot, although there are still some sponsorships, which I'll be telling you about in the guide. *Also, there are no guarantees that you will ever get a job as an Airline Pilot! But you have to look at the big picture.*

If you were setting up in business today, let's say a high street shop selling widgets of some kind. You would probably need about £30 – 50k. And that's to make an average income or maybe slightly above if you're lucky!

Most businesses make a loss year one, break-even year two and start making a profit by year three. By comparison for similar "start up" capital you are investing in yourself to be in a position to make a solid, above average income from the time that you get your first Job right through to when you retire. It's also a job that a lot of people dream about having!

If you are wondering, "how on earth am I going to fund this training without resorting to serious crime or selling a kidney?" I will be telling you about the current sponsorships and Airline Partner Programmes available, and if that doesn't work out for you then don't worry I will be giving you lots of ideas about how you can raise the money.

Most pilots start out thinking it will be impossible to fund all of this training, but where there's a will there's a way!

I will give you some ideas about planning your career. I.e. if you think you will be going straight to BA flying the Boeing 777 or similar, as soon as you have completed your training, dream on! Although occasionally you do hear about some lucky so and so that does!

I will also be including an appendix with sample questions from the Airline Transport Pilot License (ATPL) written exams. I'll also be including typical Interview questions including technical, aptitude, and psychometric test questions. I will include a typical simulator profile. Don't worry about this all sounding very scary, it will become clear as you progress with your training.

In summary you will learn about the obstacles that you will have to climb along the way from:

- Learning whether it is a career that you really want.

- The training and qualifications that you require.

- How to get through the training effectively, and with the minimum of pain, whilst saving a fortune.

- How to put a good CV together.

- Learning how to get an interview.

- Learning how to pass the Interview.

- Preparing for, and how to pass a simulator assessment.

- Sample questions.

- Preparing for Line Training.

- And Finally, Career Planning.

So get yourself a cup of coffee and we'll start off by talking about what it's really like being an Airline Pilot.

CHAPTER TWO

WHAT IS IT REALLY LIKE BEING AN AIRLINE PILOT?

One of the first things I realized when I first became an Airline Pilot, was that I was so absorbed in becoming an Airline pilot that I didn't do any real research in to what it is actually like being one. I was in for a shock!

The first shock to the system, was that I was a person used to being self-employed, going to bed late and getting up around 8 am every day. Suddenly I had no flexibility for a "lie in"

I had to be in bed early and up very early – 3.30/4 am- and was suddenly horrified to find that half of my new working life would be spent doing this! YUK! At the time of writing I'm in to my eighth year with the airlines and can tell you, honestly, that I still dislike earlies. Some love them, but oh no not me! You do get most of the day to yourself but I argue that's no good if you're tired out for the rest of it.

Of course the other half of the story is that you will be reporting around midday, or close to it, and work an afternoon shift. This means finishing in the evening around 8-9 pm typically which means again most of your day is wiped out, when you are working, your social life is virtually non- existent if you have a busy roster! I work for a regional airline - mainly because I like to get home most nights - and live in my home town, where I want to be. And this is about the closest to 9-5 that you'll get in the Airline Industry too!

Some of you will work at the freight airlines i.e. DHL which will typically involve you reporting in the evening and flying through the night. Again you will have to adapt to a large change in lifestyle because of this. You will be staying "down route" in hotels all over the World for periods of 3/6 nights per week or more.

The corporate lifestyle may suit others among you whereby no fixed roster exists more like a tranche of hours set by to be on call. You get a call during those hours if your employer wants you to fly them somewhere. Some have more of a roster some have no roster at all and expect you to be ready at will. A kind of 24-hour stand by. This is generally more haphazard in terms of a stable lifestyle and will involve periods of night stops away from home, all over the world.

Then there are the charter airlines i.e. Thomas Cook, Thompson fly etc.. Where again you could be reporting for work at very strange hours of the morning to fly through the night. Again expect night stops.

Whichever route you chose you will have night stops and will have to get used to spending your life living out of a suitcase! Regional and low cost airlines have far less night stops, however they do occur.

On the plus side it's usually great fun, and you can quite often have a nice trip or tour, visit some really nice places and have some great laughs along the way. It's a great lifestyle for younger people generally, but some of the older ones like it too! I could write another book about aircrews "down route" which would be a fun read I'm sure, but I'll leave it there for now. I'm sure you can imagine though!

The previous paragraph touches on a very important aspect of being an airline pilot. It is so important that airlines spend a lot of time and money carefully interviewing and assessing candidates to ensure that they will fit the mould. That is the candidate's personality. It is so important that you are the type of person that is easy going and capable of getting along with all types of people.

Obviously the main reason is that you will be spending a lot of time with these people and if you are the type of person that don't like folk and prefer to be on your own, or down the pub with the local numpties, and no one else then it really isn't for you, so do something else! Ideally you will be a friendly outgoing and stable type of person, no good if you have the emotional intelligence of a hormonal teenager for obvious reasons!

During selection you will probably do a personality questionnaire, I have included sample questions in chapter seven of this book. The airline industry and the C.A.A Civil Aviation Authority have worked out that the ideal Candidate will be a stable extrovert! So that is "ideally" what they will be looking for in your tests and during interview. Conversely the ideal long haul pilot is a stable introvert. Don't get all hung up with this though. It really is a mix of personalities, and again I would say the main thing is that you can get along with people easily. I'm sure that one of the main things Airline

Interviewers consider during interview is the question "could I be locked in a flight deck quite happily with this person for 8 hours or more?"

In my experience there are many wide and varied types of people in this industry with all sorts of different backgrounds. I've flown with ex: firemen, policemen, soldiers, shopkeepers, window cleaners, truck drivers, businessmen, cruise ship workers, civil servants (I was one too) financiers, geologists, journalists, salesmen, surveyors, IT consultants, butchers, builders, plant machinery workers, school teachers, musicians, footballers, and so on. I think you get the idea! Flying attracts all sorts of weird and wonderful people!

So by now, hopefully, I have given you a flavour of the type of people and lifestyle you will experience being a pilot, *and by now you should have realized that it is very different to a lot of careers - you will have to work your life around your roster!*

You will, obviously, have your qualifications by then, which I will cover in the next chapter. Therefore you will have a good idea of your role on the flight deck as an airline pilot. Although you will still have a lot to learn!

You will start your career in the classroom doing an aeroplane type conversion (if you haven't done so prior to joining the airline) you will have a lot of study, learning about the aeroplane that you will be flying, followed by a simulator course and skills test. Once this is done you will start your "line training".

This is very challenging yet enjoyable, as you will be flying an airliner for the first time. You will typically do 40/50 sectors (1 sector = airport to airport) of training followed by a test called the "Final line check" it's just to make sure that you are safe to operate with "normal" line Captains as opposed to Training Captains.

So once you're "signed off" to the line you are an airline pilot. And that day you will be grinning like a Cheshire cat!

I'm sure that you are intelligent enough to know that this is a mentally demanding role, which is the reason that there needs to be a lot of discipline on the flight deck.

The line training previously mentioned addresses this required discipline. The "Standard Operating Procedures" or SOP's are the rules of operation - if you like. You will be taught how and when to action the appropriate check list.

To give you an idea of what I mean I'll give you a brief outline of a typical day at work for me:

TODAY'S DUTY: BRISTOL TO BRUSSELS, BRUSSELS TO BRISTOL, BRISTOL TO BRUSSELS, BRUSSELS TO BRISTOL.

BRS-BRU-BRS-BRU-BRS report time 11.10 UTC

10.50: Arrive at Bristol airport, report to company crew room.

11.00: Print weather pack, notams (notices to airmen) journey log and OFP (operational flight plan) Check for company memos/"Stop Press" and notacs (notices to air crew) technical and/or operational, check aircraft performance, and check them all, carefully!

11.10: Report to company operations department (Ops) by telephone. Obtain info regarding passenger loads, operational requirements I.e. aircraft swap, Add's (Aircraft acceptable deferred defects) ATC (air traffic control)Slots, crew changes, requirement for de icing (winter) etc...

11.15: Brief first officer and cabin crew regarding all of the above. Conduct an interactive crew safety briefing such as: everybody's duties should an emergency decent be carried out.

11.25: Liaise with ground handling services to arrange required fuel uplift, catering and passenger load. Confirm required: taxy fuel, trip fuel, pantry code, crew composition, aircraft DOW (dry operating weight) and any ballast. All required to produce the aircraft load sheet. Arrange crew transport if necessary.

11.35: Arrive at aircraft, conduct "walk around" of the exterior and conduct internal checks to prepare for an on time departure at 12.10 UTC.

11.50: Board passengers, check performance, PF (Pilot Flying) either the captain or first officer, briefs PNF (Pilot Not Flying) about the departure, and then carry out checks before starting.

12.00: Welcome on board briefing to passengers via P.A system. Obtain clearances from ATC.

12.05: Pushback and start engines five minutes early.

13.00: Arrive in Brussels 15 minutes ahead of schedule having carefully followed company SOPs (Standard Operating Procedures) for each phase of the flight: before starting and after starting engines, taxying, lining up on the runway, take off, after take off, altimetry procedures, cruise, planning descent and arrival, descent, approach and landing, after landing, parking and shutting engines down.

13.15: Conduct turnaround checks. Conduct "walk around" visually inspecting the aircraft exterior. Liaise with dispatchers as previously.

14.15: Board passengers bound for Bristol. Check aircraft performance, PF briefs PNF about departure. Carry out before start checks.

14.25: Welcome on board PA to pax. Obtain clearances.

14.35: Still waiting for ground starting crew to arrive at the aircraft.

14.45: ground crew finally arrive, push and start Clearance obtained. Pushback and start engines ten minutes late as a consequence.

15.45: Arrive in Bristol on schedule after negotiating a nice shortcut from ATC. SOP's as per previous sector.

16.10: Depart Bristol as per previous occasion.

17.15: Arrive back in Brussels as previous occasion.

19.05: Depart Brussels on time after another long turnaround deliberately so arranged for connecting passengers.

20.00: Arrive back in Bristol after shutdown checks, call ops (operations) to confirm aircraft status and any crew changes to next duties. Arrange crew transport back to crew room.

20.15: Arrive back in crew room. For each sector, input fuel uplift, fuel burn and flight data required for emissions into the computer. File days duty envelope.

20.30: Duty ends, after a long, tiring yet enjoyable day, drive home. Out of base tomorrow operating Heathrow to Hanover and back 16.15 UTC report.

11.10-20.30 a 9 hour and 20 minute duty plus a 1-hour drive each way makes a long and tiring 11hrs 20 min day (not allowing for the 20 minutes early in the crew room).

To give you a brief introduction to SOP's and the use of a normal checklist I have included an A320 Normal Checklist below.

A320 Normal Checklist

DEPARTURE

BEFORE START

Cockpit Prep . . . . .Complet (Both)
Signs . . . . .On/ Auto
Adirs . . . . .Nav
Fuel Quantity . . . . ____ Kg
To Data/ V. Bugs . . . . ____ Set (Both)
Baro Ref . . . . ____ Set (Both)
Mobile Phones . . . . .Off
A/Skid & N/W Steering . . . . As Rqrd
Windows/ Doors . . . . Closed (Both)
Off Beacon . . . . On/Auto
Thr Levers . . . . Idle
Parking Brake . . . . As Rqrd

AFTER START

Anti-Ice . . . . As Rqrd
Ecam Status . . . . .Checked
Apu . . . . As Rqrd
Pitch Trim . . . . ____ Set
Rudder Trim . . . . Zero
Ground Crew . . . . .Clear
A/Skid & N/W Steer Ing . . . . On

BEFORE TAKEOFF

Flight Controls . . . . Checked (Both)
Flt Inst . . . . Checked (Both)
Briefing. . . . . Confirming
Flap Setting . . . . Conf____(Both)
V1. Vr. V1/Flex Temp . . . . ____(Both)
Bump/ Derate. . . . . As Rqrd
Atc + Tcas. . . . . Set
Radar + Pws. .Secured For To
Cabin . . . . To No Blue
Ecam Memo. . . . . Auto Brk Max
                                                         Signs On
                                                         Splrs Arm
                                                          Flaps To
                                                   To Config Norm
Laptop . . . . .Stowed
Strobelights . . . . As Rqrd
Cabin Crew . . . . Advised
Eng Mode Sel. . . . . As Rqrd
Packs . . . . As Rqrd

AFTER TAKEOFF/CLIMB

Ldg Gear . . . . Up
Flaps. . . . . Zero
Packs . . . . On
Baro Ref . . . . ____ Set (Both)

ARRIVAL

APPROACH

Briefings . . . . Confirmed
Confirmed Pins & Covers . . . . Removed
Ecam Status . . . . .Checked
V. Bugs . . . . Set (Both)
Seat Belts . . . . On
Baro / Mda /Dh . . . . .____ Set (Both)
Eng Mode Sel . . . . As Rqrd
Autobrake . . . . As Rqrd

LANDING

Cabin Crew . . . . Secured And Advised
A/ Thr . . . . Speed/ Off
Go Around Alt . . . . ____ Set
Ecam Memo . . . . .Ldg No Blue
L/G Down
Signs On
Splrs Arm
Flaps Set

AFTER LANDING
Consider Adverse Weather

Flaps . . . . Retracted
Spoilers . . . . Disarmed
Apu . . . . Start
Radar/Tcas/Pws . . . . Off/Stby
Strobe Lights . . . . Auto

```
PARKING

Apu Bleed. . . . . . . . . . . . . . . . . . . . . . . . . . . . . . . . . . .  On
Engines . . . . . . . . . . . . . . . . . . . . . . . . . . . . . . . . . . .Off
Seat Belts. . . . . . . . . . . . . . . . . . . . . . . . . . . . . . . . . .Off
Ext Lt . . . . . . . . . . . . . . . . . . . . . . . . . . . . . . .  As Rqrd
Fuel Pumps . . . . . . . . . . . . . . . . . . . . . . . . . . . . . . . .Off
Park Brk And Chocks. . . . . . . . . . . . . . . . . . .  As Rqrd
Capt's Mobile Phone . . . . . . . . . . . . . . . . . . . . . . .  On
```

```
SECURING THE AIRCRAFT

Adirs . . . . . . . . . . . . . . . . . . . . . . . . . . . . . . . . . . . . . . .Off
Oxygen. . . . . . . . . . . . . . . . . . . . . . . . . . . . . . . . . . . . .Off
Apu Bleed. . . . . . . . . . . . . . . . . . . . . . . . . . . . . . . . . . .Off
Emer Exit Lt . . . . . . . . . . . . . . . . . . . . . . . . . . . . . . . .Off
No Smoking . . . . . . . . . . . . . . . . . . . . . . . . . . . . . . . . .Off
Apu And Bat. . . . . . . . . . . . . . . . . . . . . . . . . . . . . . . . .Off
Laptop . . . . . . . . . . . . . . . . . . . . . . . . . . . . . .  Secured
```

CHAPTER THREE

HOW DO YOU START
YOUR JOURNEY?

Well folks before you start any training you need to know if you are medically fit enough for licensing. I recommend that if and when you decide to go ahead with training, that the very first thing that you do is book the (required) class 1 medical exam at the CAA Gatwick www.caa.co.uk I discuss this in more detail at the end of Chapter 7. Best to make sure that you pass before spending a lot of time and money! Although you don't have to be Superman/Wonderwoman to pass, it is quite a detailed exam. Check the CAA website www.caa.co.uk for details and current fees.

If you want to become a commercial airline pilot in Europe you will need to obtain a Commercial Pilots Licence with an Instrument Rating (CPL/IR), and you must have the Airline Transport Pilots Licence (ATPL) ground exams passed. This is called a "Frozen" ATPL until you qualify by experience - 1500 hours Total Time with 500 hours Multi Crew Experience

– when the CPL/IR becomes "unfrozen" and the ATPL is issued. The ATPL is the highest level of aircraft pilot licence. You need an ATPL to be a Captain of an Aeroplane weighing above 5700kg or with over 9 passenger seats.

The licensing authority in Europe is currently the JAA (Joint Aviation Authorities (very soon to be EASA- European Aviation Safety Agency) and is administered in the UK by the CAA (Civil Aviation Authority) The licence issued is technically called a JAA CPL/IR and JAA ATPL respectively. By the 1st July 2012 they will be called EASA CPL/IR and EASA ATPL respectively.

Just to repeat to help it sink in, because it is slightly mind boggling with all of these strange letters, a certain level of experience is necessary 1500 Hours Total Flying Time (TT) including 500hrs Multi Crew (Airline Experience) and 100hrs flying at night, before you can get your ATPL issued. Initially, you will have a Commercial Pilots Licence with Instrument Rating (CPL/IR) issued at 200 hours, which is known as a 'Frozen' ATPL when the ATPL written exams are passed.

Note that you can work as a First Officer for an airline with a Frozen ATPL.

There are two routes "approved" by the authorities that you may take to obtain a frozen ATPL:

1. Integrated Route

2. Modular Route

Each route has its pros and cons. But you must review your own individual situation and choose which suits your circumstances better.

INTEGRATED V MODULAR ROUTES

The integrated route is currently available from Oxford, Atlantic Flight Training, CTC, FTE Jerez and WAAC in Australia and will cost between £70,000 and £95,000.

It will take you about 14 months and is a continuous course of training, where the ground school and the flying is totally integrated, and completed by the same school. You end up with a frozen ATPL. Some Airlines tend to prefer integrated students and some of the current Airline Partner/ "Sponsorship" packages (All mentioned later) include integrated courses. However the most common route is the modular route because it's cheaper and more convenient for most students.

The UK modular route is available from about 20-30 approved schools in the UK (and the States) and will cost you anything between £30,000 and £60,000 – For the same licence! Modular training can be completed at different schools.

As the name suggests the training is split into modules. I have included approximate costing's:

1. PPL (Private Pilots Licence)- £7000 Inc. test fee

2. ATPL Ground School - £3000 Inc. exam fees

3. Hours building to 150 hours - £10500 (USA)

4. CPL (Commercial Pilots Licence) - £7200 Inc. test fee

5. MEP Rating (Multi Engine Piston Land Rating) – £3000

6. IR (Instrument Rating) – £15,300 Inc. test fee

7. MCC (Multi Crew Co-operation course) - £3000

Approximately £49,000 including JAA/EASA written exam

fees, flight test fess and aircraft hire for tests. Then you have accommodation, flights and loss of earnings/living costs to factor in on top. Allow at least another 10 – 15% for unforeseen items i.e. failing exams, extra training, bad weather etc.... What's that? An extra £10-15,000? Making it £60-£65000 all in, depending on your cost of living etc.!!

The modular route is much more flexible than the integrated route, in that you can do it in your own time-scale (2/3 years is common) and, therefore, spread the cost better (although it can, like the integrated route, be achieved in 14 months if you do one module, immediately followed by the next). In addition, there are other advantages such as being able to do the ground studies by distance learning, or doing the flying training on a part-time basis so that you don't have to give up your day job.

Important: You must complete the ATPL written exams within 18 months of your first sitting, using a maximum of 6 sittings and no more than 4 attempts at an individual paper within the 6 sittings. The 18 months period is counted from the end of the month of the date of the first sitting. The papers can be attempted in any order. Achieving at least 75% of the marks allocated to that paper would award a Pass in the examination.

You only have 36 months from the date (rounded up to the end of the month) of passing your last ATPL written exam in which to get your CPL or your IR issued. If your CPL *and* IR are not granted within the 36-month acceptance period then the ATPL theory credit will lapse. You will be required to re-pass all of the ATPL exams to regain ATPL theory credit. However, if you've previously passed all of your ATPL exams but were not granted a CPL/IR within the 36-month acceptance period, the amount of ATPL theoretical knowledge instruction you

need would be at the discretion of the Head of Training of the Approved FTO. ATPL ground exams are valid for a period of 7 years from the most recent validity date of the IR entered in your CPL. Check LASORS on the CAA website www.caa.co.uk for up to date legislation. Not a major issue if you have a clear plan to get on with your Training, Have all of your courses mapped out and booked.

Remember though **NEVER PAY FOR ANY AVIATION COURSE IN FULL UP FRONT**. I have seen some very big schools go bankrupt – a long standing UK Integrated Flying School has just gone bust at the time of writing after taking lots of students payments in full for courses they were never going to get. Lots of Flying Students have lost lots of Money – You Have Been Warned!!! Pay As You Go!!!

WORKING THROUGH THE MODULAR ROUTE

So, how do you go about getting your frozen ATPL through the modular route?

You start off by booking a trial flying lesson 30 minutes/ 1 hour, at your local airfield, to see if it's something you will really enjoy doing!!?? Then if you're completely hooked get yourself a Pooleys JAR-FCL Professional Pilots Flying Logbook. Then start your PPL Private Pilots Licence, a 45 hour flying course with a test at the end and with some straightforward written exams. It's a little bit like the car licence in a way, because once you have it you can take your friends and family up for a ride in a little two/four seater aeroplane (you can't make money from flying until you have a CPL) This can be done in the UK or abroad; in fact it does not even have to be a JAA/EASA PPL it can be an ICAO PPL (available from most other countries in the world).

If you are planning to go to the States to do a PPL – beware of schools that offer you a guaranteed PPL in three weeks. The level of training is generally poor and the test tends to be just a 'tick in the box'. This is a bad grounding for a career in aviation. In addition, if you have weather problems you may not finish your course so you will either have to stay on in the States (cost of changed air ticket, additional accommodation costs, more time off work etc.), or have to come back to the UK and try and finish over here which, depending upon how bad the training was in the States, may mean having to do a complete course again.

Once your PPL has been issued, you have two parallel routes to follow:

1. Your ATPL ground school (which you can do by distance learning or full time study).
Distance learning gives you the benefit of being able to keep working but you have to be fairly disciplined, setting aside a specific number of hours per week, and not allowing distractions like going to the pub with your mates! Bristol Ground school www.bristol.gs do a mixture of distance and classroom learning which they call blended learning.

2. Structured hours building
Hours building can be done in the UK or abroad. Many have done this in the USA (typically Florida) as it is usually much cheaper and the weather is usually great. It would take somewhere between 4 – 6 weeks depending on the amount of hours that you need. Hard work but great fun!

At this point, I would like to make a couple of recommendations about your hours building:

Don't just fly around the same airfields time after time. Try to vary your flying. Go away for a few days. Land on grass

runways. Land at airfields within control zones as well as your local field. Practice the exercises in the CPL syllabus!*

As mentioned previously, do some hours building abroad; it can be thousands of pounds cheaper in the States, South Africa, and Australia. If you are just hours building in the States (i.e. not training) you do not need to use a JAA approved school. In fact, their aircraft availability is sometimes not too good and they tend to be more expensive than an FAA school. You will have to get an FAA PPL issued first, which is just a paperwork exercise, a small fee and a flight test.

Try and fly different types of aircraft if you can afford it. Why not try a tail-dragger? Perhaps do some flying in a complex single, or possibly even a multi-engine aircraft...

NIGHT RATING

Whilst hour building, at the same time, do your night rating. It's 5 hours flying at night 4hrs with an instructor and 1hr on your own including 5 solo full stop take offs and landings, which is required for CPL issue.

FOR THE CPL (COMMERCIAL PILOTS LICENCE) MODULE:

In order to start your CPL training course, you need to have 150 hours total time (TT)

In order to take your CPL or IR skill test you need to have passed all of your written exams.

In order to get your CPL issued you need to have the following:

---

* www.caa.co.uk, Personnel Licensing, Standards Document 3, Applicants Guide for the CPL Skill Test

- 200 total hours including

- 100 Pilot in Command hours

- 5 night hours including 5 solo full stop take-offs and landings at night

- A cross-country flight of 300 nm with stops at two airfields other than the airfield of departure.

You should note that if you do your IR after your CPL, you can get 10 hours dispensation on the required course hours (making it 45 hours rather than 55 hours), although you need to have 'met all the requirements for CPL issue' before starting.

FOR THE IR (INSTRUMENT RATING) MODULE:

There are no minimum hours requirements to start your IR, although you do have to have a night rating, but I would, strongly recommend, not bothering to start the IR module until you have done the CPL module. It is without a doubt the most difficult module!

In order to get your IR issued you need to have 50 hours Pilot in Command cross-country flying, and you must have passed the written exams. Before you start the IR get RANT XL Release 3 (Radio Aids Navigation Tutor) from http://www. oddsoft.co.uk/rant2000.html Its excellent! It will give you a massive head start! Also, prior to starting get your hands on the aircraft power settings, SID'S, STAR'S and Approach plates that you'll be flying on the course/test and practice using Microsoft Flight Simulator.

TRAINING FOR YOUR MULTI CPL/IR

As mentioned previously the total cost of this training is around £25,500 (depending upon how you do your training), split roughly into just over £10,200 for the CPL and Multi Rating and just over £15,300 for the Multi IR. The CPL Module is usually done in a single engine 4 seater such as a PA28 Arrow, to keep the cost down. This is a "complex type" i.e. has a variable pitch propeller and retractable landing gear. Alternatively the CPL can be done on a Multi- Engine such as a PA34 Piper Seneca. The Multi Rating (MEP) is done prior to the IR. The IR will be done partly in a simulator and partly in a Multi-Engine aeroplane, again, such as a PA34.

MCC COURSE

In order to get your frozen ATPL and to be able to apply for a job as a First Officer you have to do a Multi Crew Co-operation course. This can be done on a turboprop or a jet simulator and will cost between £2,000 and £4,000.

The following Flowchart gives you a simplified version of the various stages to the training.

Flowchart shows the minimum requirement to become an Airline Pilot in Europe.

> PRIVATE PILOT LICENCE PPL
>
> 45 hrs total
> 35 hrs dual
> 10 hrs solo
> Skill Test

STRUCTURED HOUR BUILDING

Build up to 173 hrs total time
To include 100 hrs P1 before starting CPL course

NIGHT QUALIFICATION

5 hrs total
4 hrs dual
1 hr solo

ATPL THEORY

650 hrs theoretical Knowledge
14 examination papers

COMMECIAL PILOT LICENCE CPL

25 hrs dual
Skill Test with CAA examiner

MULTI-ENGINE RATING MEP

6 hrs dual
Skill Test

INSTRUMENT RATING IR

50 hrs dual
Skill Test with a CAA examiner

> MULTI-CREW CO-OPERATION COURSE MCC

> FROZEN AIRLINE TRANSPORT PILOT LICENCE FATPL
>
> "Unfrozen" by combination of type-rating and multi-crew hours

SUGGESTIONS BEFORE COMMENCING YOUR FLIGHT TRAINING

I will be covering the selection of Flight Training Organisations (FTO's) fully in the next chapter, but before I do I would like to make a recommendation that you take a good look at the schools I suggest below before you decide on your school(s) The following are UK Flight schools that have a good reputation for quality training and good pass rates. **I must emphasise that I am not personally recommending** any Flight School, ATO or FTO and that you should do your own due diligence when selecting Flight Schools. As I will repeat throughout this guide: Don't pay upfront for any aviation course! If you must do then try to arrange a third party Escrow account through a solicitor. Flying Schools can, and do go bust very quickly!

APPROVED TRAINING ORGANISATIONS (ATO'S) OR FLIGHT TRAINING ORGANISATIONS (FTO'S) WITH AIRLINE PARTNER PROGRAMMES

The following three Establishments (CTC, OAA and FTE Jerez) are known as ATO's or FTO's and are approved by JAA/EASA and the necessary local authorities for their client and partner

airlines. They each have Airline Partner Programmes, which in turn have different selection criteria. I will not be covering them all in this guide. Visit their websites or call them to learn all about them. Their Airline Partners will look to take pilots trained by them first and foremost! They are:

1. CTC for integrated training and the CTC Airline Cadet Programme.

CTC have Airline partnerships with BA, Monarch, FlyBe, Easyjet and others. The general consensus among several of my colleagues, currently, seems to be that you have the best chance of getting placed with an Airline after completing the CTC Cadet programme. For full details of this visit their website. *If I were just starting my journey, I would be checking these out first for sure! Book on to one of their open days, and take a good look!*

http://www.ctcwings.co.uk/

2. Oxford Aviation Academy

http://www.oaa.com for Integrated and Modular Training. They are not the cheapest, but in the opinion of many, they are *simply the Best!* Several Airlines, *in addition to* their Airline Partners, prefer OAA Trained Pilots. They have several Airline Partner Programmes.

3. FTE (Flight Training Europe) Jerez

http://www.ftejerez.com/ for Integrated and Modular Training, FTE Jerez has several Airline Partner Programmes.

For FTO's (Flight Training Organisations) with a proven track record:

Airways Flight Training Exeter

http://www.airwaysflighttraining.co.uk
Modular Training with good pass rates and excellent for "pay as you go!"

Bristol Aviation
http://www.bristol-aviation.co.uk
Modular Training with good pass rates.

Atlantic Flight Training Coventry
http://www.flyaft.com
Integrated and Modular Training, good pass rates.

Bristol Ground school
http://www.bristol.gs
ATPL Ground Exams Training. Alex Whittingham has an excellent reputation! And the school has very Good Pass Rates.

CHAPTER FOUR
WHICH FLIGHT SCHOOL(S) SHOULD YOU CHOOSE?

What should you be looking for in a school/FTO?

Naturally, things such as location, costs, your selected training route etc. will influence your choice. If you are among the lucky ones who benefit from sponsoring, then you don't have to make a choice. All that work would have been completed for you.

Always visit the school before you decide. Try not to be fooled by glossy brochures and the like. Be sure to check things out for yourself and don't be afraid to ask questions. After all, you're going to hand over a lot of dosh to this establishment. What is the use of high tech. training equipment, if the teaching levels are poor?? Therefore, don't rush this part; this is an important process on your journey. A hurried decision made here, could cause dire consequences later.

I have put together what I will call a checklist of points/

questions to ask etc. In the future, working to a checklist will be a constant part of your working life, so lets get used to it now:

MY CHECKLIST

- How long has the flight school been in business?

- What are the classrooms like?

- What are the credentials of the Instructors? Are the instructors young students, trying to build their hours to join an airline? Aim for the highest level of instruction, you deserve it.

- What is the schools reputation on safety & regulation policies?

- How many and what type of aircraft are used for training?

- Does the school offer any additional benefits such as financial aid or housing?

- What is the pass rate?

- What is instructor to student ratio? You need to ensure that there is capacity for you to fly every day; otherwise your costs will soar.

- How long does it normally take to complete the CPL Module/IR Module?

- How can I pay for my training and what are the refund policies? This is an important question, as some schools allow you to "pay-as-you-go" whilst others expect the whole payment upfront. AVOID ANY SCHOOL THAT REQUIRES UPFRONT PAYMENT.

I know people who have lost £50,000 and more paying upfront. Flying schools (And Airlines!) tend to go bankrupt, so watch out. If you have to pay upfront, ask if you can have a third party Escrow account arranged through a solicitor.

- Can the school give assistance with employment?

- Find out exactly what is included in the course quotation. Many schools do not include things such as examination entry fees, flight test fees, accommodation, travel to overseas and things such as these. These extra costs can add up very quickly, so save yourself a nasty shock and make sure that you know.

- Are progressive flight checks given? These checks serve to appraise your progress during the training.

- Will your training be properly planned and managed by the school? Ensure that you will be under the supervision of a member of staff who will oversee your training and progress to the end.

- What would happen if weather/maintenance problems forced lessons to be cancelled? Who would be responsible for reporting maintenance problems and rescheduling of lessons?

Remember, there are plenty of flight schools to choose from. So if you get a bad feeling, and things just don't seem right... They're probably not! By using a methodical approach, you will find a school that suits your needs and personal character. Be determined not to settle for poor quality. Most of all, don't be shy, ask questions if there is something that you don't understand and speak to the students that are already there!

CHAPTER FIVE

HOW DO YOU RAISE THE FUNDS NEEDED FOR YOUR TRAINING?

Don't worry; I'm not going to get you involved with any illegal or unethical schemes to get the cash! However, initially, it may seem that raising the cash could be the largest hurdle on your career path. And the average training course could set you back between £40-60,000 or even more.

The financing will depend on the route you take. For example: If you manage to get selected by a participating Airline Partner with OAA or FTE Jerez for the Multi-Crew Pilot Licence (MPL) programme, the Airline *may,* possibly, pay up front for your training, which would, probably, then be paid back from salary on employment, depending on the agreement.

AIRLINE PILOT SPONSORSHIPS.

Sponsorships are currently available in the Far East, and the Middle East with a lot of the national flag carriers. Currently,

they are taking applications from their own national citizens. The Cathay Pacific Cadet Sponsorship is open to all, visit their website www.cathaypacific.com for details. By comparison, sponsorships are virtually non-existent (in the traditional sense at least) in the UK today. Nowadays, the Airlines realise that they have an eager and ready supply of people who are prepared to pay their own way in order to get on the ladder. Coupled with the harsh economic climate, this has continued to make the situation harder for new pilots. However, there are still a few limited opportunities available in the UK! There is a full Sponsorship programme, with all training paid to Frozen ATPL and a guaranteed first officer job at the end flying with West Atlantic Airlines. Their requirements are: Current JAA PPL, current class 1 medical, UK driving licence and the right to live and work in the UK. Naturally, the competition is intense. This is the only "genuine" sponsorship remaining that I am aware of in the UK.

For further information about West Atlantic Airlines Sponsorship, speak to Hilary at Propilot on +44(0)2476 511447, email: hilary@propilot.eu or visit: http://propilot.eu/your-career/west-atlantic-cadet-scheme You will be able to download an application form from the site.

For Airline Partner Programmes/"Sponsorship":

British Airways, BA Future Pilot Program.
http://www.bafuturepilot.com/

CTC Wings
www.ctcwings.co.uk – mentioned previously

Oxford Aviation Academy
www.oaa.com - mentioned previously

FTE Jerez
www.ftejerez.com - mentioned previously

THE MPL (MULTI CREW PILOT LICENCE)

This is a new JAR/EASA Licence that has been designed for pilots to be trained more directly in terms of a specific Aircraft Type and Airline S.O.P's, and geared specifically to a particular Airline. It is more simulator focussed (therefore cheaper) I understand that at the time of writing this course is being offered through Oxford Aviation Academy and FTE Jerez and trains students put forward by several Airlines including; BA, Flybe, Easyjet and Dragonair. I also understand that a few of these Airlines are funding a small number of students with a view to being paid back from salary over five years, on appointment as a Pilot. It is a new licence and seems to have a mixed response in the industry. Is this the way of the future or just a nine days' wonder?

If you have decided to choose the integrated or the modular training route, then this means that you will be expected to raise the funds yourself. The beauty of modular training is you can spread your training over a longer period of time. This allows you to work between modules, enabling you to keep debt to a manageable level.

Here are some ideas for you to mull over. Just remember that you may have to try a combination of two or three of the ideas found here. But the point is to get creative. Where there is a will, there is a way:

Try to find any training grants offered by the Government, some local government funded "charities" could possibly be able to help? If you dig deep enough, you may unearth some surprises! The grant may not cover all of the costs, but I'm sure you'll agree, that every little counts towards your dream. In addition, a grant doesn't need to be paid back!

Research if there are any Government Career Development loans available. They become available from time to time.

Check out grants offered by non-Government organizations. These too, do not have to be repaid.

Some banks offer professional development loans. At the moment, Barclays and the Co-operative banks are offering attractive benefits. Some form of security will be required. Think carefully about this, as your house could be at risk if you are unable to keep up with the repayments.

Get a credit card. Some flight students, use a credit card to pay for some or all their flight training financing. But do shop around. Several credit cards have many advantages over the traditional loans. These include, cash back and many months zero interest rates which you can move around and use to your advantage.... however, if you are in the history books for not paying off credit and debts, you will struggle to get one.

Get a private loan from your parents, relatives or friends. Picking up a loan in this way is much easier, especially if you know the right people. And you will probably find that the interest rates will be much lower than if you had taken it out with a bank. To make this option more attractive to your loved ones, you could maybe get an additional part-time job, and arrange for your salary to be paid directly to their account? The point I'm making is, get creative, you will find a way! I'm still amazed to this day about how I managed to find the money to do all of my training!

If you are in your teens or early 20s, here is another idea for you:

Flying Scholarships. These scholarships are generally aimed at young people (teens and 20 somethings..), and funded by an aviation organization. The scholarship offers students the possibility of flying experience ranging from a few hours to a full PPL.

Here are a list of all the flying scholarships, (including their website links), currently available in the UK:

Glen Stewart flying scholarships
http://www.flyingscholarship.co.uk/

GUILD flying scholarships
http://www.gapan.org/career-matters/scholarships/

The Air League flying Scholarships and Bursaries
http://www.airleague.co.uk/scholarships/

RAFA scholarships
http://www.rafa.org.uk/images/library/files/Flying_
Scholarship_Application_Form_2010.pdf

The great thing about scholarships is that you never have to pay them back! For that reason it's clear that competition is fierce. You've got to be "in it to win it" so have a go, apply for everything along these lines if you're eligible. Applying for this kind of scholarship includes filling out and sending an application form. This is followed by a formal interview (please take note of the tips in the interview section of this guide). An aptitude test may also be included. Its important to note, that all applicants are required to be medically fit up to class two standard. But as mentioned at the beginning, if you are going down the ATPL route get your class 1 medical first before you do anything else!

Extra Tips for your CV in connection with Scholarship applications
Make sure you include the heading, "Extra Curricular Activities." Mention everything you do that involves teamwork. For example, get involved with the Duke of Edinburgh Awards.

Education. If you are lucky enough to find yourself at school, try to get good grades at maths and science. This will definitely boost your application.

Finally, if you fail at the interview, try, try, again! Your strong determination will reap success for you. And it would also impress the interviewer.

These ideas for financing should get your "gray-matter" working. Please think long and seriously about this aspect, as mistakes made in this area, can live with you for a long time to come. I cannot stress highly enough, the importance of careful financial planning. Good luck....

CHAPTER SIX

YOUR CV – YOUR ADVERTISING TOOL

Before you run off to dig out that CV you designed when you were at school or college, one thing needs to be absolutely clear: Your CV has just around 15 seconds to prove itself, so you need to get it right the first time round. If you want your CV to stand out from the crowd, follow my ten Top Tips:

1st Top Tip. ALWAYS include your photo with your CV application. A head and shoulders shot in the top right hand corner should be enough. Remember, the photo will probably be the first thing that attracts their attention, so make sure it's professional and presentable. Otherwise your CV could end in the rubbish bin.

2nd Top Tip. Never send a solo CV (unless specifically requested). Prepare a well written cover letter. This will act as an "Ad" for your CV. Use this letter to emphasise skills that set you apart from your peers. I will be writing more about

this later in the chapter.

3rd Top Tip. Make sure there are no grammatical errors or spelling mistakes in your CV. Believe me, an automated spell-checker does not guarantee that your document is free from errors.

4th Top Tip. You stand a better chance, if you tailor your CV to the airline you are applying for.

5th Top Tip. Your CV should not be longer than one page. Try to remember that it is a life summary, not your autobiography.

6th Top Tip. Try not to use a font smaller than 10 points. And avoid using fancy font types. Just stick to one type. And please, no coloured paper.

7th Top Tip. Avoid using negative expressions, such as, "unfortunately," "no experience........"

8th Top Tip. Make sure that there are no gaps in your CV. (for example, in your work history) You will need to prove your history for the last 5 years, otherwise you will not get a UK Airport Security Pass. My Airline had to fire a new entrant First Officer recently, because he couldn't prove his last 5 years work history!!! He'd made it all up, Doh!!!

9th Top Tip. Before sending your CV, get someone to proofread it.

10th Top Tip. Avoid sending your CV in a hand written envelope. All modern printers are able to cope with printing on envelopes. This is a chance for you to discover buttons on your printer you never knew existed!

CV STRUCTURE

Your CV is a concise and handy summary of your flying credentials and will often be used by the interviewers during the interview.

As I mentioned earlier, your airline pilot CV is very different to the "every day" stuff. It will need to be written specifically with "flying" in mind. So it's a good idea to include any management, leadership or relevant technical skills from previous employment. Your flying story to date should be clearly mapped out.

Your CV will generally consist of 7 headings:

1. **Objective:** mention the specific position you desire within the airline.

2. **Certificates & Rating:** In this heading, you should first state the type of licence and rating you possess i.e. EASA CPL/IR. Next, mention your medical, Instructor Rating and other relevant qualifications.

3. **Flight Times:** Make sure these are exact timings. This summary should be for; total time/pilot-in command/ second-pilot-in-command/instructor pilot/Multi-engine/ single-engine/turbojet/ turboprop/ Instruments/

4. **Flight Experience Special Training & Achievements:** Here you can mention, major ground and flight schools that are connected to your important positions, rating and licences.

5. **Education:** Under this heading, emphasis should be placed on college or university training.

6. **Availability:** Let them know by what date you would be available for the new position.

7. Interests Include this heading then you could state here, for example any language or IT skills that you possess. Also any other technical abilities. List also any involvement in sport that reflects teamwork.

I strongly recommend that you join BALPA www.balpa.org as a student pilot. It's free and you will get lot's of great quality info' about CV's and interviews for free!

Another option is to check out pilot bookshops. A good book that I came across is, "Airline Pilot Interviews: How You can Succeed in getting Hired," written by Irv Jasinski.

The Cover Letter
Try to keep this letter short and to the point. It is the tool you can use to introduce your CV. Use a conversational writing style and avoid using that "I" word too much. Lets look at the typical structure of a cover letter:

The Heading
This should compose of your contact details, name, address, telephone number and email address. leave your MSN or Skype name out.

The Receiver
A letter addressed to a person, makes a better impression than does a generic one. So try to find out the name of the recruiter. You may find this information on www.pilotjobsnetwork.com on their website, or a pilot forum such as www.pprune.com Finally, you could ring up the company's switchboard and ask the operator for the name of the person who deals with recruitment. Make sure though that you get the correct spelling, otherwise your efforts could end up in vain.

For a list of every AOC (Air Operator Certificate) holder in the UK – Including every UK Airline, large and small, visit

www.caa.co.uk/aocholders

You can then use www.pilotjobsnetwork.com or www.pprune.com to find out the contacts, criteria etc....

The First Paragraph
This should state clearly the reason you are writing to xyz Airline. Two or three sentences are enough. Also state your objective and that you have enclosed (or attached, in the case of email) your CV.

The Body
In this section you can highlight the desired pilot profile of

The Airline. Tell the recruiter the flying experience you have and how it may be relevant to the role, i.e. some Airlines seem to prefer Integrated Students, some seem to prefer Flying Instructors, trained at Oxford etc.... Make sure you point this out to them here.

The Closing Paragraphs
Close your letter with a statement promoting you as a strong, capable candidate for the position. The close should contain a discreet request for action, such as; "I look forward to meeting you in the near future," or "please forward an application form." Finish off, by signing your name personally with a contrasting ink colour.

Just in case you are having problems coming up with those perfect phrases for your cover letter. I have complied a helpful list of specific pilot cover letter phrases that will assist you in writing an effective cover letter:

"I am writing to express interest in a position as..."

"Your company's reputation as the most punctual regional airline has prompted me..."

"Enclosed for your review is my CV which briefly outlines my experience and education"

"I would welcome the opportunity to..."

"Solid career progression"

"For more than five years I have flown extensive _____ operations"

"I have extensive experience..."

"The following are highlights of my qualifications;

My experience includes;

Relevant to your needs, I offer: (bullet points follow these phrases)"

"Your company's exciting new fleet of _____..."

"My greatest strength (asset)..."

"I am confident that my experience and education to date provide me with the skills that would benefit your airline"

"My experience, professionalism, and enthusiasm..."

"I am confident that my background in flying _____ makes me a qualified candidate for your First Officer position..."

"I would like to meet with you and discuss my skills and background and how they would contribute to your company's needs..."

"I offer strong team leadership and effective communication skills..."

"I'm excited about the future of XYZ Air and am eager to contribute to its growth..."

"Thank you for your consideration. I look forward to hearing from you."

Before I finish this chapter, Id like to, again, draw your attention to a supportive organisation that would be well worth joining. Its called British Airline Pilots Association (BALPA). You will find them at: http://www.balpa.org. And it's free to join if you are a student pilot. You will receive lots of current information about airline contacts, recruitment procedures, interview advice. CV writing tips, salaries. And every year, they organise a recruitment conference, where representatives from almost all airlines in Britain are present. This can give you the added benefit of meeting up and talking with them about their current recruitment plans.

There is also the Flyer Magazine Annual Professional Flight Training Exhibition, which has many UK Airlines and FTO's in attendance. In the words of the event organisers, it's an "Absolute must for anyone considering a career as a professional Pilot" I've heard nothing but praise for this event!

CHAPTER SEVEN
THE INTERVIEW – YOUR ROUTE TO SUCCESS

I'm sure you've worked out by now that it is very difficult to get a job as a pilot! There are people that have gone through all of that training and financial hardship that have never got a job flying. Most people do seem to get a job, but not always straight after qualifying. It is all a gamble! But if you follow the advice in this guide you will be stacking the odds heavily in your favour!

In my opinion, getting the interview in the first place, is probably the hardest hurdle. Apart from the Sponsorships and Airline Cadet programmes previously mentioned, do not apply until you have your licence you will just be wasting your time. When you have it though apply to as many airlines as you can. You will really have to get busy posting; don't miss a single AOC (Air Operator Certificate) holder out.

For a full list of AOC holders in the UK visit www.caa.co.uk/

aocholders Apply for the small jobs as well as the big ones. Then after a week or so get on the phone and follow them up. Keep an Airline contacts book with every Airline listed and the date of every single letter, phone call, email, CV, contact name, notes of any conversation etc. that you send.

In line with tradition, UK airlines start their hiring process in the autumn. This ensures that they have the necessary number of pilots for the following peak summer period. This means you should endeavour to plan your training so that you can finish by the end of summer, and get going with sending your CV, making follow up calls, and all the necessary things outlined in this chapter. Note that recruitment departments will normally ring to arrange an interview, so it is of the utmost importance that you are contactable. If not, they will just go on to the next person..."opportunity lost!" I had that happen to me once!

Airlines change their requirements at very short notice. So just because you didn't meet the requirements last time, doesn't rule you out forever. Stay in touch! I cannot emphasise enough, the importance of networking. Airlines may have thousands of applications on file from budding pilots. The way for you to stand out from the crowd is by having an "INTERNAL RECOMMENDATION." So get networking and try to meet someone who works for the airline you want to work for – preferably a Training Captain or a management pilot if possible, and stay connected. I know people who got jobs because they became aircraft dispatchers or Cabin Crew to get themselves on the "inside" You have to think outside the box!

WORK HARD TO GET INTERVIEWS!

Draw up a plan for contacting so many Airlines per week, by telephone, websites, email and so many by CV and Covering letter. Work your leads and try to build a steady rapport with your contacts. Don't get lazy, work hard to get yourself interviews! Most importantly though, you must Network. You will often hear the phrase in aviation "It's Not What You Know, It's Who You Know" How true it is! Get to know Pilots within or on the fringes of your social circle. Use Facebook, Twitter, and MySpace etc. Get creative and you will get an interview! Do nothing and you will get nowhere!

WHEN YOU GET AN INTERVIEW

When you do get the call for an interview you will be excited to say the least! You will then need to get back down to earth quickly to get thoroughly prepared for it. Different Airlines have different recruitment procedures. A "Biz Jet job" may be just a chat and a simulator assessment, whereas a large Airline might have a detailed two-day selection process including some or all of the types of tests I'll be covering in this chapter. You MUST do an interview preparation course BEFORE you attend the interview GEARED TO THE AIRLINE THAT IS INTERVIEWING YOU!! This will help you to develop the fundamental skills and methods you will need for the relevant airline pilot assessments and interviews. The course will give you the edge over the other applicants.

It's possible that you can do a course that can be completed by e-learning from the comfort of your own home and at your pace. All you need is a computer and an internet connection.

They are at e-interviewpreparation.com. They offer a 15 hour interactive e-course, equivalent to a 4 day seminar. Their

course has won awards for aviation quality. Find out more information and course content at:

http://www.e-interviewpreparation.com/pilot/learning.php

Although, in my opinion, I think you would be better to do a structured Interview preparation course with a well established professional, one on one.

Believe me; you won't regret doing a preparation course. It will help you nail that interview. Once you know you have an interview pending, (and only then please) contact me at frozenatpl@aol.co.uk I will give you further assistance, advice and give you the number of a brilliant contact that has helped hundreds of people pass Airline Interviews with most UK Airlines, (including myself) this is reserved for you as a thank you for buying my guide. Keep it to yourself though! Competition is fierce remember!

In the meantime, research all you can about the airline you have an interview with...Who are the key figures? Find out important facts about the organization. Read annual reports. Review the information on their website, check www.pprune. com , check www.pilotjobsnetwork.com Check Google News and see what the world has to say about the company. Google is a powerful research tool. Use It! Just remember that KNOWLEDGE IS POWER. So learn all you can about them.

YOUR IMAGE

It goes without saying; mistakes in this department will be costly to you. An airline pilot is expected to present a professional appearance to the public. So do wear a well-fitting suit in black, or grey. Hair should be neat and tidy. And for men, a short hair cut is best.

A genuine smiles, direct eye contact and a firm handshake shows confidence. No one wants to shake hands with a dead fish. Would you feel confident about a dead fish grip on the controls of a plane? Very unlikely...

Be punctual. This is essential for a pilot. So if you have never been to the location before, check it out in advance and save yourself any embarrassment.

Aviation is a very small world!!! People get to hear names very quickly if there is a reason to!!! Therefore, try to be pleasant to everyone you meet in aviation and try to make a good first impression.

Try to find the "Gouge." This is the phrase used to define information complied after the interviews, from both the successful and the unsuccessful about what they experienced

during the whole process. Many airlines produce their own gouge on their site. Google the information and once again, do not be afraid of doing research. You will find a lot of information in the "wannabe section" on www.pprune.com a Pilot Rumours and News Website (lots of good info' regarding Training and Exam Requirements too). Be careful what you believe regarding some of the posts, there may well be some exaggerations! There can be a lot of negative posts too, try not to get "sucked in" Stay focussed and stay Positive!! Also, again, lots of airline insider info at www.pilotjobsnetwork. com

THE INTERVIEW STARTS - ORIENTATION

The first part of the interview will consist of an orientation. This will include a short overview of the airline and a detailed description on how the interview will be conducted. You will also be introduced to the staff that will be involved with the

interview. If time allows, they may also answer any questions from applicants. This is a sterling opportunity for you to make

a good first impression. In your preparation, you would have researched the company, its history, stock info, current operations etc, so by your questions, you can show the interviewer(s) that you have made an effort to get to know the airline. But make sure not to over do it!

THE LOGBOOK REVIEW

This is probably the most basic part of the interview, but could turn into a nightmare, if your logbook hasn't been correctly maintained. So make sure your logbook is neat, kept up-to-date and that in no case, have you tried to exaggerate anything. Any mistakes in the logbook should be clearly corrected and initialled. Double check that your calculations are correct. This is certainly not a task to do at bedtime on the eve of the interview. Prepare in advance.

HR INTERVIEW

A human resources officer and a management pilot will normally conduct this. During this part of the interview, the interviewers will be asking certain questions and are looking for acceptable answers that will help them evaluate if you are what they are looking for in terms of a co-worker and an employee. Once again this is the perfect opportunity to sell yourself! You will be asked how you got into flying or a similar question along those lines. This is the chance you've been waiting for! Tell them your whole flying story so far (you would have prepared and rehearsed this umpteen times, so it will come out naturally – this is exactly what I did!). This will take up a good 10-15 minutes of the interview. You will feel

relaxed, initial nerves will vanish and interviewers will be glad for a chance to sit back and have a break. Bear in mind that they've probably been interviewing all week, so this will be a refreshing change for them not to have to work as hard, and they will probably warm to you as a result!

Here are some typical background questions that you could be asked:

BACKGROUND QUESTIONS

- Which job have you enjoyed the most and what reasons?

- What are your hobbies?

- What are your two major weaknesses?

- What makes you angry?

- Other than flight training, what have you done to prepare for this course?

- What can you bring to xyzair?

- What do you like about flying?

- What will you do if you're not successful on this occasion?

- Why do you want to work for xyzair

- Tell me about the decisions you made at school to improve your chances of becoming a pilot.

- What do you think are the important qualities of an airline pilot?

- Where do you see yourself in 10 years time?

PSYCHOLOGICAL QUESTIONS

- Tell me about a time when you had to make a decision involving the safety of others?

- How would you settle a conflict with a superior?

- How would you handle a situation involving an abusive passenger?

- What would you do if you smelt alcohol on your Captain's breath?

- Your Captain attempts to go below your DA on an ILS Approach and you are not visual, what will you do?

Additional Tips

Don't worry if you have to pause before giving an answer. This is good. It shows you are thinking about the

answer, which is a bonus. And make sure when you answer, that you use a confident tone. Remember to be open with the information and "sell yourself" with each answer.

Honesty is the best policy! They are trying to assess two main things: (1) You are the kind of person they would like to fly with, (2) You'll have no problems with the initial training. They just want to see that you are a nice guy/gal who can get on well with others and do a good job.

TECHNICAL TEST QUESTIONS

Naturally, they will want to be assured of your technical knowledge in relation to the job. (You will probably not understand any of the questions below until you have done your ATPL Ground School) here are some sample Interview Technical questions, they could be aural questions, a written

paper or a combination of both:

- What function do leading edge slats perform?

- What is Dutch Roll?

- Does altitude affect stall speed?

- Why does tailwind increase take-off roll length?

- Explain the reasons for differing engine positions on aircraft i.e. why do some a/c have engines on wings & some on fuselage?

- Why does a/c have swept wings?

- What are the advantages of a super critical aerofoil?

- What effect does altitude have on Mach number?

- Two aircraft are flying at different levels, same Mach No, which one would have the Higher TAS?

- What is coffin corner?

- What is the purpose of a Mach Trim system?

- What are the advantages of Variable incidence tail-plane?

- What are 6 reasons for Spoilers?

- What are the stall characteristics of a swept wing aircraft (& a T – tail?)

- What are the advantages of a T-tail?

- What are the main differences between the flight characteristics of jet and turbo –prop aircraft?

- What do you know about Icing procedures…hold over times etc??

- When does clock start??

- Describe RVSM levels? Describe MNPSA levels?

- Briefly describe the ICAO cruising Levels?

- Name at least 6 differences between flying at FL250 & FL350?

- What inputs to GPWS are there? And what modes are there?

- What is EGPWS?

- What is the difference between a base turn & a procedure turn?

- Describe the black hole effect? Why is it potentially dangerous?

- What is the effect of weight on a glide?

- Describe high speed flight area?

- What are the advantages of FAN engines?

- What is Jet upset?

- What is PRNAV?

- What is BRNAV?

- What engines does the Embraer/Airbus/B737 have?

- What disadvantages of T-Tail a/c?

- What is the difference between an ERJ 145 & 135 or A319/A320? (depending on which type you will be flying)

You will be expected to have a good understanding of the following:

- LOW DRAG

- Momentum & inertia....VITP

- Speed margins

- Poor lift at low speeds

- Yaw & roll dampers

- Sweep

- Mach No & theory

- Stall qualities

- The general handling of jet aircraft

- Mach trimmers & high speed flight

I would like to encourage you to get hold of the following book(s):

Ace the Technical Pilot Interview by Gary v. Bristow

And for students wanting to pursue a career with Cathay Pacific: **Preparing for your Cathay Pacific Interview, The Pilots Guide, by Captains X,Y and Z**. This is a source of technical interview questions for many other airlines too!

Finally, **Handling the Big Jets by D.P. Davies**, is also a great book, and will help increase your technical knowledge.

PSYCHOMETRIC TESTS

These tests fall into two categories, namely, (1) **personality questionnaire** which attempts to measure various aspects of your personality. Try to be honest here, nothing can be gained by trying to be someone you are not. And, (2) **aptitude** tests, which attempt to measure your intellectual and reasoning abilities.

PERSONALITY TEST

These tests gauge your personality by asking about your feelings, thoughts and behaviour in a variety of situations. Depending on the duration of the test, you may need to answer between 50-250 statements. You will have to answer each one on a scale of 2, 5 or 7. (I.e. 1 being not like me, and 5 being exactly like me).

Here are some examples:

- Do people who are inefficient anger you?
- Do you like to first plan a task?
- If you are criticized before others, do you feel bad?
- Do you prefer to avoid arguments?
- Do you prefer to do a task alone?
- Do you care what others think of you?
- Do you prefer facts?
- Do you donate to charity regularly?
- Do you feel more comfortable doing one job at a time?
- Do you gain pleasure from trying to make sense of the meaning of art and poetry?
- Are you affected if one of your friends is in trouble?

Then there are simple a) or b) type answers:

I prefer to avoid conflict.

a) True   b) False

Another style of personality questionnaire:

I enjoy parties and other social occasions.

a) Strongly disagree b) disagree c) agree d) strongly agree e) Neutral

Work is the most important thing in my whole life.

a) Very strongly disagree b) strongly disagree c) disagree d) agree e) very strongly agree f) strongly agree g) neutral

APTITUDE TEST

This is a computer-based test and normally lasts around 90 minutes. The test covers: Hand-eye co-ordination/multi-tasking/memory test/situation awareness/mental arithmetic. The aptitude test will also include the Psychomotor Test, and you will be shown into a room and sat down at a computer with a joystick. The test will measure your ability to make sense of information in two dimensions, so as to achieve a solution in a three-dimensional form.

Using your joystick, you have to position a dot onto a pattern, which is moving in a random manner on the screen as it scrolls down. At the same time, you are required to control the "rudder" of the plane with your feet. This task is designed to evaluate if you have the ability to complete several tasks at once. Therefore, the longer you can position the dot on the set pattern, the higher your score will be. In the final analysis, the test determines whether you have the natural aptitude to fly an aircraft.

THE PSYCHOMOTOR TEST PROFILE

As I mentioned above, you will be seated in front of a desktop computer with a joystick. You will also have a mouse and mini keyboard. The test composes of 5 parts:

1. There will be a static cross at the centre of the screen and you'll have to control two lines (vertical & horizontal) with your joystick. To move the horizontal line you must either pull the joystick back or push forward. And for the vertical line, you move it either left or right. Because of the virtual 'wind factor', the two lines will be moving continually. The aim is to steer the two lines together so that they will both come to be upon the static cross. This test consists of three parts. All three parts of the test are similar and the scores range from 1 - 10 for each part of the test.

2. This is a test of your observation. Here, you'll have to wear a set of headphones and use the mini-keyboard as the main input device. You'll get three men standing in four positions (facing you, back facing you, upside down facing you, and upside down back facing you). Each of them are holding either a round or square object in each of their hands. A voice from your headphones, will ask you how many of them are holding either a round/square object on which hands. So your answer would be either all three of them (keypad number3), two of them or one of them or it could be none of them. This test has a time limit.

3. Once again, for this test, you'll be using the mini-keyboard as the main input device. You'll get two very untidy diagrams, and you are given an 'X' shape at the bottom. So for each area of the test, you'll have

to define whether the 'X' shape could be found on the 1st diagram or the 2nd diagram or even both of the diagrams. You'll have a time limit of 30 seconds.

4. For this test, you'll be using the mouse to click on the objects. You'll be given a table of co-ordination. There are around five or six rows and five or six columns each. The rows represent the colours and the columns represent the shapes. For this test, there are two similar parts. It should be noted that, the rows of colours, and columns of shapes are constantly changing.

5. For this test, you'll be using a joystick again. Believe it or not, you'll be virtually flying an aircraft! The only thing is, you will have to fly into the trail of boxes that are coming towards you. This test composes of three parts and the score ranges from 1 - 10. A word of advice, move the joystick GENTLY!

MEMORY TEST

The memory test evaluates the short-term memory and tolerance for stress. This is a test of your ability to detect relevant information, whilst being distracted by similar but irrelevant information. This is the kind of thing, which can typically occur in a cockpit environment.

Here is a great site where you can practice to your hearts content: http://www.the-biomatrix.net/bionew/memory-test. htm the memory game on this site is very straightforward. You just click to start and then memorise the numbers that appear on the screen. After ten seconds they will disappear, and then you write your answers in the boxes and click to check your answers as you go along. Have fun!

NUMERACY TEST

This includes, basic arithmetic, number sequences and simple mathematics. Here are some typical questions:

What number is the next number in the sequence?

$$16, 32, 64, 128, \_\_\_$$

•

Which number is larger: 0.8, 8, 90, 250?

•

When simplified (2.43 × 2.43 + 2.43 × 7.57 × 2 + 7.57 × 7.57) is equal to:

(a) 10   (b) 100   (c) 101.89   (d) 200.59

•

Three years ago, the average age of A & B was 18 years. With C joining them, now the average age becomes 22 years. How old is C?

(a) 24 years   (b) 27 years   (c) 28 years   (d) 30 years

•

The average age of 8 men is increased by 2 years when two new men replace two of them whose ages are 21 years and 23 years. The average age of the two new men is:

a) 22 years   (b) 24 years   (c) 28 years   (d) 30 years

•

John sold an umbrella for ` 680, losing 15%. The cost price of the umbrella is:

(a) ` 782    (b) ` 800   (c) ` 578   (d) None of these.

From the teams competing in the world swimming championships, 20% are from Europe, half as many are from the USA and one twentieth are from Africa. What fraction of teams are from neither Europe, the USA or Africa. Is it,

(a) 13/20   (b) 17/20   (c) 15/20   (d) 13/15

•

If a cup of pancake mixture makes 2 pancakes, how many pancakes can be made with 3 cups of pancake mixture?

•

An aircraft flies at 400 nautical miles per hour. How long will the aircraft take to travel 100 nautical miles?

•

A litre of petrol costs £2.50. How many litres of petrol can be purchased with £8.00?

SPATIAL REASONING TEST

Your spatial ability will also be tested. This is the ability to manipulate shapes in two dimensions, or to visualize three-dimensional objects presented as two-dimensional pictures. Sample questions:

If a gear on a motor turns clockwise, and is attached to another gear, which direction will the other gear turn?

•

Which of the following shapes has the least drag, if thrown in the air:

Square, Rectangle, Circle, Polygon, Triangle

VERBAL REASONING TEST

The main purpose to this test is to establish how competent an applicant is in their understanding of written English. And to evaluate their ability to deal logically with written information.

Here are some sample questions:

Assume the first two statements are true.

1) A girl has a car

2) Car drivers have driver's licenses

3) Drivers Licenses are green

Is the final statement true, false, or indeterminable?

•

Michael goes cycling or hiking every day. If it is snowing and windy, then Michael goes hiking. If it is sunny and not windy, then Michael goes cycling. Sometimes it is snowing and sunny.

Which of these statements must be true:

a) If its not sunny and its snowing then Michael goes hiking

b) If its windy and Michael doesn't go hiking, then it is not snowing

c) If its windy and not sunny, then Michael goes hiking

d) If its windy and sunny, then Michael goes hiking

e) If its snowing and sunny, then Pedro goes hiking

To help you become more proficient in doing the above kinds of tests visit www.how2become.co.uk there are lots of great

verbal reasoning, numeracy, aptitude, psychometric, spatial, symbol rotation tests etc.... that can be done online under timed conditions. It's a very effective way to practice. By practicing you will get good at doing them

THE FLIGHT SIMULATOR ASSESSMENT

I need to mention here that each simulator assessment is different. But this profile will serve as a guide and useful tool, to help you be prepared as to what to expect at your assessment. Also I must point out that the following information ***doesn't represent any particular aircraft and has been completely made up, in order to give you an idea*** *of a typical simulator assessment.*

This part normally lasts about an hour.

Remember, the goal of the airline is to see how flexible you are in adapting your skills to something new – they want to see that you will be able to get through the type rating course. (Be aware that the airline may conduct the simulator in an aircraft that they don't fly themselves). They will watch how you brief the approach; how you cope with mistakes (and how you learn from them) they will be looking for a high standard of Instrument Flying. Your scan must be nice and sharp for this.

Handy Tips
At the briefing, take a deep breath, compose yourself, and listen carefully to the instructions given. Don't miss out on important numbers, speeds, power settings and such like. If in doubt, ask!

Be well prepared! Contact me (ONLY WHEN YOU HAVE A SIM' ASSESSMENT PLEASE) frozenatpl@aol.co.uk about a

simulator prep' course – STRONGLY RECOMMEND THAT YOU DO ONE!! It will massively help your chances if you do!! Use Microsoft Flight Sim' to help your scan! There's an add on for virtually every type of aircraft now. Use RANT Radio Aids Navigation Tutor, to revise holds etc....

A Typical Simulator Assessment

The XYZAIR simulator assessment will incorporate the following exercises:

- General handling

- Take-off and climb

- Radar vectored ILS to land.

- Engine failure during flight

- One engine inoperative ILS to land

The XYZ Aircraft simulator will be flown from the right hand seat.

The flight director and auto-throttle will not be used.

The training captain who completes this assessment will occupy the left seat and will act as a competent Pilot Not Flying (PNF). He will NOT provide any training input, but he will answer any questions you have before starting the detail. He will not debrief you at the end of the session.

AIRCRAFT CONTROLS

Steering

Rudder pedal steering provides control throughout the initial part of the takeoff and latter stages of the landing run.

Trimmers

All aircraft trim controls are electric. The horizontal stabiliser trim switches are on the outboard part of the control wheel.

Airspeed Indicator

The analogue airspeed indicator includes a digital readout. There is 1(orange) internal airspeed cursor and 4 (white) external bugs. Selecting the required speed onto the mode control panel operates the orange cursor – this will be done, on command, by the PNF.

Electronic Attitude Indicator (EADI)

The EADI is a standard presentation. Bank angle is indicated at the top of the EADI and is graduated in 10-degree increments. Thirty degrees of bank is to be used for turning manoeuvres. Pitch graduations are labelled every 15 degrees, sub-divided every 2 degrees. A speed tape is located to the left of the attitude display.

MFD Multi-Functional Display

The Multi Function Display (MFD) presents radar, TCAS, FMS, CMC and other navigation information and systems pages.

Altimeter A conventional altimeter is fitted with a moveable index to bug decision altitude.

Vertical Speed Indicator (VSI)

The VSI is a standard presentation. Indications are derived from the inertial reference system so that the readout is instantaneous.

Radio Management Unit (RMU)

The Radio Management Unit consists of a display and a bezel panel that provides control of the communications and radio navigation equipment. Additional airplane systems

information is also available on specific RMU selectable pages.

FLIGHT DETAIL

You will board with engines running and before takeoff checks completed. The aircraft will be positioned at the threshold of runway 23R at Manchester. You can expect a brief familiarisation of the flight deck instrumentation.

Takeoff and climb thrust is 86% N1.

You will be cleared for takeoff and climb initially on runway heading to 4000 ft. Ask for takeoff thrust to be set and maintain the runway centre-line with rudder pedal control. At Vr rotate at 3 degrees per second to 16 degrees, and with a positive rate of climb call "gear up." Climb at V2+15 kts to 1000 ft agl and then lower the nose to 11 degrees to give a climb rate of not less than 1000 fpm. With a speed in excess of V2+15 kts, flap retraction is initiated by calling "flap Zero." Passing 170kts then accelerate to clean manoeuvring speed.

A short general handling exercise to include turning, climbing and descending will follow the take-off.

You will then be radar vectored towards the localizer for runway 23R at 215 kts and it will be up to you to determine the best point to reduce speed. Ultimately, you will be cleared for an ILS and landing on runway 23R. The following flap manoeuvring speed schedule must be followed for deceleration:

Beginning at the manoeuvring speed of 200 kts, extend flaps to the next setting. As the flaps extend, reduce speed to 180 kts.

Flap 45 is used for a two-engine landing. And Flap 22 is used

for one engine inoperative landing.

Reduce speed to 180 kts before establishing on the localiser. Approaching the glideslope, reduce speed to be fully configured for landing as descent commences.

Following the landing, you will be repositioned final approach with both engines operating. An engine will fail and you will be required to maintain control.

To counteract overall thrust reduction, BOTH thrust levers should be advanced. To control thrust asymmetry due to engine failure, smooth rudder application is required. Finally, the rudder load is trimmed out.

The rudder is very powerful. Avoid over controlling on the rudder as the yaw will cause roll and induce pilot control wheel input. The slip indicator below the PFD must be used to maintain zero aircraft yaw.

The final requirement is to fly a one engine inoperative ILS and landing.

For a real simulator assessment - with a real aircraft type! There would be diagrams and clear examples of the profiles flown, along with thrust and attitude settings. Again you would have tables or diagrams clearly illustrating these. There would also be clear diagrams of the instruments.

GROUP EXERCISES

In this exercise, the group takes part in three exercises:

1. Practical problem solving

2. Group discussion

3. Communication and verbal reasoning.

The exercises generally last half a day, with two assessors monitoring the group closely. A typical group discussion question could be:

- How could high fuel prices affect your career as a pilot?

- How would it be possible to change the traditional image of an airline pilot?

The group could also be set various challenges:

- Discover the best method to drop food aid parcels to villages in need, via the most fuel-efficient route. Also take into account packing the goods, so that they leave the aircraft in order. Think about volume of packages etc.

- Build a bridge out of pieces of wood that could hold a cup of water.

The group would also be given exercises that test their verbal reasoning. Here are three examples:

- You find yourself stuck on an island. What items do you think would be essential for you to have with you?

- Discuss together a typical issue in the news and reach a conclusion.

- Build a bridge that would be able to support a glass of water.

Bare in mind, the assessors are looking for team skills such as listening, questioning for clarity and making statements clearly. There's no need to worry about achieving a realistic solution! Also, they are on the look out for; leadership, decisiveness, enthusiasm, a positive and supportive attitude, energy etc. Each group member will be graded on a scale

from "well below average" to "well above average."

Try hard to give a positive contribution to the discussions and above all, get to know your team and relax.

THE MEDICAL

Some airlines have their own medical examination in addition to the JAA/EASA Class One Medical Exam required by the authorities. It goes without saying that, good eyesight, hearing and general medical fitness are obvious requirements for the job.

Whilst we are on the subject it's worth reiterating at this point, that you will need a Class One Medical Certificate. **I suggest you get your medical certificate before beginning flight school or anything else. This should be your first step!!** The medical will alert you to any physical condition that could prevent you from becoming a pilot. I'm sure you'll agree, its better to find out at the beginning, rather than after spending thousands of pounds on training etc.

The initial medical must be done at the UK CAA Aeromedical Centre at Gatwick. For details of their current costs and other information, please review their website: www.caa.co.uk.

It is recommended that you allow approximately 4 hours for your appointment and wear comfortable clothing. Your medical will be quite extensive and will include such tests as ECG, EEG, cholesterol, lung function, audiogram, haemoglobin, lipid profile among others.

If you require further advice about a pre-existing condition, you can write to them enclosing a report from your personal doctor at:

CAA medical department contact details:
Aeromedical Centre
Aviation House
Gatwick Airport South Area
West Sussex RH6 0YR
Telephone: 01293 573700

They never expect anyone to be medically perfect of course, however, it is quite a detailed test. If you feel that you might have a condition that could possibly prevent you from passing the medical, give them a call on the number above or check the website www.caa.co.uk. Be sure to have relevant information/documentation from your doctor, which will assist them to gauge your condition. Good luck!

Now this chapter has come to an end, sit back and visualize yourself making it through... The airline has just phoned you to tell you the good news..........you look in the mirror and Garfield smiles back at you. You've made it! You're so high, your flying without wings! The hard work was well worth it! CONGRATULATIONS!

Visualizing your success goes a long way to you attaining it. So keep up the good work.

CHAPTER EIGHT
AIRLINE TRAINING

Having secured your dream job, you will be taught the airline's company policies and Standard Operating Procedures (SOPs). You will immediately commence the type-rating course on the aircraft that you will be flying (unless you have it already?)

TYPE RATING TRAINING

As I explained previously, the type rating on your licence permits you to fly a specific aircraft type. This part of the training will be completed in a Full Flight Stimulator (FFS) The full motion of these simulators will enable you to experience the aircraft's flight dynamics, performance and handling. The course is normally completed over several weeks, and is combined with base training, ground school and a simulator phase.

GROUND SCHOOL

This part of the program, relates to the aircraft systems and SOPs. And will include classroom sessions, some computer-based training (CBT) and usually lasts 10 days. Once you have finished this and passed the written exams (yes more written exams!), you will move onto the Simulator Phase.

SIMULATOR PHASE

This phase involves you being paired up with another student, and taught to co-operate as a team to fly the aircraft. Depending on type, the duration of this phase is about 9-12 four-hour sessions. At the end, there is a Licencing Skills Test (LST) with an approved CAA examiner.

BASE TRAINING

You now get to fly the actual aircraft that you've been training on in the simulator! The base training will consist of 6 take-offs and landings. This training completes the requirements of the type rating and the CAA can now endorse your licence with the type.

LINE TRAINING

This is the next stage after type rating has been completed. Line training can be described as "on the job training." It teaches those additional skills and knowledge needed in the day-to-day operation. A qualified training captain, who will supervise your flying up to a certain amount of sectors, will accompany you. Initially, in addition to the training captain, there will be another qualified First Officer, who will act as a safety pilot.

On completion of the necessary number of sectors and provided that you are ready, you will be put forward for what is called your "Line Check". Basically, this will consist of a sector as Pilot Flying (PF), followed by a sector as Pilot Non Flying (PNF). In this role you will be liaising with air traffic control, monitoring the flight plan and other related tasks. Another tough period of training but very enjoyable.

CHAPTER NINE
SALARY AND PERKS!!!!

Now for the chapter you've all been waiting for!!!!! After all this, I'm sure you would like to know, what's in it for me???? It's generally assumed, that pilots earn huge sums of dosh. Some are well paid. But I wouldn't expect to be the next millionaire in your first year on the job if I were you! As with any career, the starting salary can be low.

There are various underlying factors affecting a pilots pay:

1. The pay-scale of the particular airline

2. Aircraft flown

3. Length of service with the company

4. If they are a First officer or Captain

5. The hours in their monthly plan

The monthly payment of a pilot is made up of a complex sum, and may consist of:

- **Flight pay.** This is calculated by the hour, based on when the aircraft starts moving, until standstill.

- **Duty pay.** This is normally an hourly rate paid per duty hour.

- **Allowances.** Generally speaking, allowances are a fixed payment per day. The amount is dependent on factors such as, destination, length of stopovers etc. The allowances are provided to cover the expenses incurred

- **Sector pay.** A sector is the name given to describe the "take-off to landing" phase, and a fixed sum is paid per sector.

It might be interesting to note here, each airline has a set of minimum guaranteed flight hour pay in their pilot contract. Clearly, depending on the airline, this varies. But this is generally around 75 hours per month.

BALPA www.balpa.org have compiled a comprehensive list of salaries for a number of Airlines from 2011. Join as a student pilot and they will supply you with it on request. It will help you get a rough idea of what you can expect from each airline. As is normally the case, all data is supplied in good faith and no guarantee can be given of continuing validity. I have enclosed a sample table of salaries as a rough guide only! One or two of the following Airlines do not exist any more unfortunately – Aviation is fickle!!!:

Jet Airline salaries

Operator	Astraeus Airlines	British Airways	BA CitiFlyer	bmi Mainline	bmi Regional	bmi baby
Captain Basic	£67,000	£65,446	£58,108	£72,361	£56,932	£75,247
Top Scale	£71,000 Yr 5	£146,295 Yr 24	£67,282 Yr 12	£102,424 Yr 14	£65,849 Yr 10	
1st Officer Basic	£29,000*	£49,085	£35,686.00	£40,109.00	£34,984.00	£35,000*
Top Scale	£41,000 Yr 5	£65,295 Yr 24	£47,282 Yr 12	£62,424 Yr 14	£46,849 Yr 10	
Trainer - line	10%	17.5% Training FOs	5% to 7%	10%	£3,555	10%
Trainer - base	20%	18.5-22.5% Training Captains	LT above + 4.5%	17%	£13,272	17%
Flight duty pay	£2.30 per hour	£9.73 per block hour	£1.90	£2.84 per hour	£1.93 / hour	N
Tax	-	21% (was 18%)	(18%)	32%	10%	-
Overtime flying on day off	N	Capt £463.63	Capt £384.92 FO £236.39	Y	Capt £312 FO £196	£27.50 Per Night Stop

Operator	Astraeus Airlines	British Airways	BA CitiFlyer	bmi Mainline	bmi Regional	bmi baby
Sector Pay	N	£2.87 / duty hour	N	N	N	£22.90
Tax	N/A	100.00%	N/A	N/A	N/A	£7.80 tax free
Bond	N	N	?	£15,000 - 3 Yrs	C £15,000/3 Yrs FO £12,000/ 5 Yrs	
Annual Leave	30/35	42	30	42	38 - 49	30
Pension type	Money Purchase	Money Purchase	Money Purchase	Final Salary (DB&DC)	Stakeholder (DC)	Money Purchase
Contribution	Up to 6%	7% + employee contribution	9%	10%	9%	7%
PHI	N	Y	N	N	N	N
Personal accident	Y	3 x basic	-	-	-	-
Death in service	4 x basic	3 x basic	4 x basic	4 x salary	3 x salary	4 x salary

Operator	Astraeus Airlines	British Airways	BA CitiFlyer	bmi Mainline	bmi Regional	bmi baby
Private medical	N	Y	N	Y	Y	Y
Loss of Licence						
Captain	Y	£200,000	£100,000	1.5 x basic pay	£45,000	£107,363
FO/SFO	Y	£150,000	£50,000	1.5 x basic	£30,000	£64,800
Licence Medicals	Y	Y	Y	Y	Y	Y
Licence Renewal	Y	Y	–	Y	N	N
Staff travel	Y	Y	1	Y	Y	Y
Meal allowance		–	–	–	–	–
Holiday discounts	Y	Y	Y	N	Y	Y
Options / Bonus	N	Profit related	?	N	N	N
Next Pay Review		1 Jan 12	1 Jul 12	Jan 11- 2yr freeze	Apr 11- 2yr freeze	Apr 11- 2yr freeze

Additional Notes

bmi: - London weighting: Captain and First Officers £2,432.00 per annum + payment for days-off sold for £267/£403, together with flying duty pay, can add around £5,000 per annum

bmibaby: *The figure quoted is for a FO with a Frozen ATPL from final line check. All salary figures are subject to annual RPI increases since agreement.

After feasting your eyes on the above information, you probably want to now know, what kind of perks can you expect from your chosen airline? Again, these will vary according to the airline, but here is a guide of what you can possibly expect:

- Competitive pension scheme
- Life Insurance/Death in Service Benefit
- Medical Insurance
- Loss of Licence Insurance
- 4-6 weeks annual leave
- Staff travel concessions benefits
- Profit share/Performance bonus schemes
- Job security with seniority list
- Overtime and day-off payments
- Loyalty bonus
- Personal accident Insurance
- Career progression
- Schedule plan agreements
- Share schemes

Ryanair is certainly worth a mention for newly qualified pilots. Selection is handled through an agency such as Brookfield or Storm McGinley, check www.pilotjobsnetwork.com for the current recruitment process. Usually an interview/chat (you will have to confirm that you have the 27500 Euro for your type rating!) and a simulator assessment, then if all is well, its a rising pay scale until you have passed your line check when you go on to the standard rate. I know of a guy that has a pay as you fly contract with them, it seems to be the way it's headed. Visit www.brookfieldav.com and www.stormmcginley.com to see their latest vacancies. You will be set up as a self employed pilot and will be responsible for your own Taxation, costs; including uniforms, 6 monthly LPC/OPC, hotel accommodation etc.., however I'm told that the pay is well worth it, and the standard of training at Ryanair is very high. Those Boeing 737-800's sure look nice too don't they?

Be realistic at the start. You're going to have to work your socks off, you'll probably be based miles from home and will have to "upsticks" for a few years. And just think about it, the salaries may start low, but they're still much better than the average office workers pay!

The more senior you are, the larger the salary you will receive. Also the larger the aircraft the more you are likely to receive.

CHAPTER TEN
YOUR CAREER PLAN

The exciting thing about all of this is that the airline industry is a global one! For you, this means that, potentially, you have a variety of flying opportunities on offer. Here is a typical career pattern that you may wish to follow:

- Flight Instructor (FI)

- Turboprop First Officer- Command Turboprop

- 737/A320 First Officer- Command Jet

- Long Haul A330/747 First Officer

- Promotion to Captain

Starting as a flying instructor is a good beginning, as low hour pilots have the chance to build their hours and gain valuable experience. So let me give you the low down on how to become a Flying Instructor:

FLYING INSTRUCTOR (FI)

Important – One of the first things Airlines look at when considering whether to give you a call for an interview, is if you are in current flying practice or not. If you are not flying regularly, you will go "rusty" and the longer it's been the less likely you are to be called! If you haven't flown in the last 6-12 months, it's unlikely that you'll get called.

A great way to stay current is to become a Flying Instructor. I did it and I'm really glad that I did, because: I remained current, I earned income from flying for the first time (rather than paying a fortune for it — very satisfying) I was able to keep my job in the civil service going and Instruct part-time at weekends, I soon started building valuable flying hours towards unfreezing my ATPL and I learnt more about flying. *To teach is to learn twice! – old Chinese proverb.*

It is an expensive course, approx. £6500 at the time of writing, but you will be earning valuable flying experience and of course money! Not for everyone but it's well worth considering.

NEVER PAY UP FRONT FOR ANY AVIATION COURSE!!!!

Candidates for the FI Course must meet the following requirements:

- Valid UK or JAR (Joint Aviation Requirements) Pilots licence which must include a valid SEP (land) class rating or valid Single Engine Type rating

- JAR/EASA CPL theoretical knowledge examinations (or ATPL)

- If only holding a PPL, must have at least 200 hours of flight time of which 150 hours must be PIC (Pilot in Command)

- A total of 30 hours on SEP (Single Engine Piston) aircraft of which 5 hours shall be in the last six months preceding the pre-entry flight test

- A total of 10 hours Instrument flight instruction of which 5 hours may be in a Flight simulator or FNPT

- A total of 20 hours of cross country flying as PIC including a flight of at least 540km (300nm) in the course of which a full stop landings at two aerodromes different to the departure aerodrome.

Pass a specific pre-entry flight test with a FIC Instructor within six months preceding the start of the course.

Requirements for obtaining a FI Rating:

- Must hold a CPL or a PPL with all the CPL (or ATPL) theoretical knowledge exams passed

- Must hold a valid SEP rating

- Minimum of 30 hours flight training:

- 25 hours dual instruction

- 5 hours may be as mutual flying with another FI applicant to practice flight demonstrations

- 125 hours of theoretical knowledge instruction:

- 40 hours tuition

- 78 hours teaching practice

- 7 hours progress tests

- Final Skill Test with a Flight Instructor Examiner, comprising ground lectures and an airborne flight test.

Again, I am not personally recommending any FTO, but On-track Aviation http://www.ontrackaviation.com have a good reputation for Flying Instructor Courses within the industry.

TURBOPROP FLYING

Turboprop flying is also a good start for low hour pilots to build up multi-engine, multi-crew experience. Coupled with the multiple take-off's and landings and short sectors, these enable a pilot to build hours quickly, and achieve the experience they need to unfreeze their ATPL. For the full list of AOC owners in the UK visit www.caa.co.uk/aocholders

SELF-SPONSORED TYPE RATING

Once you have your "Frozen" ATPL (CPL/IR issued with ATPL written exams passed) and an MCC (Multi Crew Cooperation Certificate) you are ready to add your first Multi-Crew Type Rating.

Your ATPL will be "unfrozen" when you have 1500 Hours TT (Total Time) including 500 hours Multi-Crew experience.

In an ideal world, your Airline would pay for your Type Rating, however, nowadays, Airlines take full advantage of desperate "wannabe" pilots who are willing to pay for their own Type Training. (See previously mentioned Ryanair example!) In fact it's unfortunate that most Airlines have jumped on the same bandwagon and ask for at least some money towards the training. Usually the remainder is paid back from salary over an agreed period. If the Pilot leaves before that period has ended they will be liable to pay the outstanding balance. Typical example would be £3000 up front in cash followed by £300 Per Month taken from your salary over 60 Months.

There are some brave souls that are tempted to pay out the £20000 plus to add a nice shiny Airbus 320 or a Boeing 737 type rating to their licence, in the hope that all of the Airlines that use the A318, A319, A320 or B737 will come knocking

down their door to hire them. Very unlikely! Although it does put you in a better position, because you have the rating and would save £18000 approx. cash flow or more for the Airline if they took you on. It is a big gamble to do this kind of thing and for many people it's paid off (myself included) but for many others it hasn't!! I know of someone that bought himself a B757 type rating several years ago, that still has not got a flying job!!! A lot of it is to do with negotiating and communicating with your target Airline contacts. You have to get "entrepreneurial" with your approach!! I made my own luck, and that's what you have to do.

Also just to reiterate, a lot of new jobs will be out in the Far East, China, India and the Middle East, therefore, just an idea but, if you could maybe get a type rating deal out there, then within 2/3 years, you would be able to target the Airlines that use the same type in the UK or EU? You may end up living abroad not wanting to return to the UK like several of my colleagues have? But you will probably have to live abroad or if you're lucky, at least 100 miles or more from where you live, or if you are extremely lucky you might get a job based near your home (very unlikely to start with!). You've got to be ready to "Up Sticks" and move home!

If you're a family oriented person, or love where you live too much to consider moving, then I would give serious thought to whether this is the right career for you. You have to be prepared to spend at least a few years living away. And if you are thinking that you could get home for your days off, then yes you could, but I can tell you from experience that this is a miserable way to work. If you are married/live with your partner, then you have to have a good solid understanding between you both, about what your goals are!

Aviation is one of the worst careers for ending relationships,

mainly for the reasons above. A lot end during the training stage as well, due to the huge financial pressures! There's even an acronym for this in aviation too! AIDS. Aviation Induced Divorce Syndrome. And yes my marriage was a victim too! It's not all doom and gloom though there are lots that survive and prosper too. Like I said, I think that you need an understanding partner and good communication all the way.

Be very careful about where you do your training! If you do your homework properly you will find the right organization that will actively help to place you with an Airline. Remember though Self-Sponsored Type Ratings are a big gamble!! Although I never had a guarantee when I did my Type Rating, I had good indications from several sources that I would have a good chance, and back then the job market was much better than at the time of writing. Once again if you do go down this route NEVER PAY UPFRONT!! Pay as you go!!

You will realise, that once you have acquired the necessary experience, you will then have more control over your future. And clearly, you will have more to offer prospective employers; you may even be able to pick and choose the company you want to work for in a healthy market. You'd certainly be in a better position to draw a constructive career path.

That having been said, many pilots choose to stay on, for instance turboprops for their whole career. So your career path is a personal one, and must suit your lifestyle, family commitments, aviation market and your dreams.

You might aspire to flying larger aircraft (heavy metal) down the long haul route. Consider that such a move will probably require you to be a First Officer for several years perhaps?

Your progress to the next level (rank), is normally based on hours. Once you have gained the necessary hours as a First

Officer, you will fly in the right-hand seat till your experience and hours, entitle you for a command. I should add, this promotion is not automatic; it's gained on merit and hinges on a vacancy existing. This normally happens when a pilot retires, leaves or gets promoted.

There are benefits of the seniority list. As you work your way up this list, it can provide excellent job security to those who are firmly planted with an airline. Things such as roster bidding, command and base transfer requests, are all governed by seniority. Even redundancies are made from the bottom of the list. So loyalty to an airline certainly has its perks.

On the downside, if you decide to change your employer, you will find yourself at the bottom of the new employers' seniority list, regardless of your experience.

In my experience, airlines tend to handle promotions internally. So for most First Officers, your promotion to captain will be with your current airline. However, amongst the major carriers with various types and operations, promotion can mean moving between aircraft types and operations. You could find yourself changing base, which could ultimately affect your family.

You can apply for the position of Training Captain, once you have accumulated sufficient experience as a Captain and a position is available. At the beginning, the promotion is as Line Trainer, where you will be involved in training newbies amongst other things. After that, with further training and qualifications, a simulator training position could possibly be secured. You will start out as an instructor (TRI), but as you progress, you could possibly become an examiner (TRE). This will include training/testing pilots for their type ratings, bi-annual checks, command courses etc.

Below, I've included a summary of some typical airline rankings:

Second Officer (SO)
This is the rank a low-hour pilot gains when first joining the airline. This is an old rank and presently is used only by a couple of airlines. Promotion is usually received upon the pilot gaining enough hours experience.

First Officer (FO)
This is the more common rank of pilots found in the right hand seat.

Senior First Officer (SFO)
This is the most senior position in the right hand seat, usually secured when you are approaching eligibility for command.

Captain (Capt)
When a place becomes available a SFO or FO with the right experience, skill and seniority will undergo a command course to be promoted to Captain and will command the aircraft from the left hand seat.

Training Captain
Once qualified, the Training Captain supplies simulator and line training to new and experienced pilots.

ONGOING TRAINING AND TESTING

Just in case you thought that all the training and tests you had to do were now behind you, sorry folks, training and testing is an ongoing part of a pilot's life. It serves to ascertain that safety and quality are maintained. Here is a list of your annual requirements:

- Annual medical check – a local Aero-Medical Examiner (AME) can complete this.

- Annual line check – a normal passenger flight with a Training Captain, who will audit for procedure compliance, knowledge and currency.

- Simulator check – this is usually done every 6 months over 2 days where abnormal and emergency procedures are tested and trained.

- SEP training day(s) – safety training composing of fire and door drills, crew resource management, technical refresher, security and dangerous goods training.

MANAGEMENT POSITIONS

Management positions within the airline sometimes become available. These can range from Chief Pilot, Fleet Manager, Base Manager or Safety Manager to Pilot Managers. Pilot Managers are predominately based in the office, but will still engage in flying on the line occasionally.

Don't forget other avenues that are open to you as a holder of a CPL/IR. Namely, flying for a private owner, ferry flying, banner towing, bush flying in remote areas and agricultural flying. Here are some more ideas to get you going:

Air Taxi
There are several types of GA (general aviation) jobs that you can aim for once you have your CPL/IR. For example a few of the schools in the UK that do IR (Instrument Rating) training are also AOC (Air Operator Certificate) holders and use typically small twin piston engine aircraft like the Piper Seneca or the Cessna 310, to do Air Taxi work. I remember, one of my friends getting a Job with the organization that

he'd trained with flying a Seneca for them from East Midlands to Dublin most nights, flying important documents, for example. The pay is not great, but you are keeping current, your Instrument Flying is staying sharp and you are building "command" experience. (When you interview for an airline job they are looking to see that you will be a good captain in the future! Although you will start your Airline career as a first officer, Airlines only ever employ future captains!)

Air Ambulance

Similar to the above type of operation are those that carry human organs that are time sensitive and will be used in life saving operations. Also, I used to fly with a guy that flew an Islander for the Police. I have a friend that used to calibrate the ILS (Instrument Landing Systems) by flying a specialized Beech King Air into different airports all over Europe. There are a few of my current colleagues that used to fly Cessna Twins doing Aerial Survey work. All of the people I've mentioned above are now Airline Captains! It's a good stepping-stone to the Airlines.

THE GLOBAL AIRCRAFT FLEET

The global fleet will almost double within 20 years A large number of pilots will be required to fill the forecast global fleet (Information Source: The Boeing Co).

Aircraft manufacturers are selling more planes than ever. Many of those planes are going to parts of the world where operators are very short of pilots. As the world's commercial aircraft fleet is expected to double over the next 20 years, airlines are facing a serious shortage of pilots, especially in India, China, Asia overall and the Middle East.

EMPLOYMENT PROSPECTS

After the current recession, which it is hoped, is only a temporary one, the commercial airline industry is slowly resuming its recovery rate to restructure and rebuild fleet levels. This is starting to impose strains on the skilled labour market. Demand for fixed wing and rotary wing pilots, cabin crew, maintenance engineers and other support personnel is progressively increasing again, with implications for the whole industry, suppliers and other industrial sectors.

FLYING INTO RETIREMENT

Flying into retirement can certainly prove to be a golden opportunity. Airline retirement varies from 55 to 65. However, for most Europeans, age 60 has been the normal retirement age. The remaining, final salary airline pension schemes can be attractive. They are normally focused on achieving 1/3 of your salary after 20 years or ½ after 30 years.

Once you have retired from your career in aviation as a pilot, things needn't end there. There is the opportunity to move into the instructor role, and inspire trainees with your experience.

CHAPTER ELEVEN

PLAN OF ACTION!

So you have read the information in this guide, had a 30 minute/1 hour trial Flying lesson at your local airfield to make sure that you are going to love flying *(I know of a young lady that paid in full for an integrated course, to discover that shortly after starting the course that she didn't actually like flying aeroplanes and was hoping that flying would grow on her!)* and you have decided that you are going to be an Airline Pilot! Cool!

Your plan of action is as follows:

1. Get your class 1 medical booked with the C.A.A

2. Get a Pooleys JAR FCL professional pilot-flying logbook

3. Join BALPA as a student pilot – free

4. Do your PPL if Modular. Book Integrated Course if not. (If integrated disregard steps 4 – 10)

5. Do ATPL ground school straight after PPL, I recommend Alex at Bristol Gs

6. Do structured hour building in the USA when PPL and written exams passed

7. Do CPL Course on return from states

8. Do Multi engine rating straight after CPL skills test pass

9. Do IR straight after Multi Engine Rating. Get CPL/IR (FATPL) Licence issued.

10. Do MCC straight after passing IR skills test.

Once you have your PPL issued you should aim to get your life organised so that you can book all of the courses up (I Repeat - Don't pay up front!) over the following 12 - 18 Months. Allow extra time for weather, exam failures, flight test failures etc... (If you go to good schools, these should be kept to a minimum) Allow an extra 10 – 15 % to your budget also for the same reasons!! Have a clear-cut plan to your training.

Important – I'm not going to lie to you here! You will have to work very hard every step of the way; it's a really hard slog! If you think you can just turn up and the licence will fall into your lap – dream on! It will take a lot of discipline and commitment from you every step of the way no matter how bright you think you are. You will really have to want this to get through it. I saw a few people fall by the wayside when I was training. They just hadn't got the motivation that you need, missing ground lectures and generally lackadaisical with their approach. They wasted a lot of time and money, and there was no way that they were going to get through. Work hard, keep focussed, work your training plan and you will get through!

Below are some excellent resources to help you before you start training and to help you to find work once qualified:

www.flightglobal.com

It's a good idea to subscribe to *Flight Safety International Magazine* to keep aware of the industry, Aircraft Orders, Expansion etc… There is also a jobs section! Their website has a lot of aviation jobs listed. A lot of Airline Pilot Recruitment Agencies advertise with them.

Ppjn or www.pilotjobsnetwork.com

This website is provided to help students at pilot schools and experienced pilots to find information on pilot jobs. Whether you are looking for specific airline pilot jobs or more general information on piloting careers, pilot schools, pilot interviews, type rating requirements, pilot salaries and airlines, this website can help. Coverage of airline pilot opportunities is provided for many countries and airlines, and you can search by aircraft type if you have a type rating and are looking for specific pilot employment opportunities. Students at pilot schools may wish to visit the website periodically to keep up to date with the latest recruitment news for pilot jobs.

Another Pilot Jobs website, lesser-known but very good is **www.coffeelovesmilk.com** and **www.balpa.org** I've already mentioned is a great source of information. As is **www.ipapilot.com** The IPA (Independent Pilots Association) is also free to join for student pilots and has lots of useful info about JAR/EASA Pilot training, and valuable recruitment info.

I really hope that you have enjoyed finding out about how to become an Airline Pilot. If you do go ahead, keep this guide and refer to it as you progress through each stage. Be careful, there are some unscrupulous flying schools out there, it's easy to get lured, especially if you think you might save lot's

of money. Remember this "THERE ARE NO SHORTCUTS IN AVIATION" cheap and poor quality training will always catch up with your wallet down the road! There is a standard that you have to reach, poor training early on will be very expensive to correct later on in your training!!! Be careful when you choose your school(s)

I very nearly got took by a conman! I was lucky that somebody tipped me off before I, very nearly, gave a lot of money to a school ran by a crook, that made a habit of going bankrupt and running off with all of his students' cash! I've seen a lot of people burn lots of money in aviation, unnecessarily. I've given you some great schools, contacts and websites in this manual; you are streets ahead of the majority of your peers already, armed with this information! Follow the "Plan Of Action" above and get going!

Whichever route you choose I wish you the very best of luck, and sincerely hope that you enjoy your career.

ABBREVIATIONS

CAA – Civil Aviation Authority

JAA – Joint Aviation Authorities

EASA – European Aviation Safety Agency

ICAO – International Civil Aviation Organisation

JAR– Joint Aviation Requirements

FCL – Flight Crew Licence

PPL – Private Pilots Licence

NPPL – National Private Pilots Licence (UK Specific)

CPL – Commercial Pilots Licence

ATPL – Airline Transport Pilots Licence

FATPL – Frozen Airline Transport Pilots Licence

IR – Instrument Rating

IFR – Instrument Flight Rules

IMC – Instrument Meteorological Conditions

VFR – Visual Flight Rules

FI – Flying Instructor

IPA – Independent Pilots Association

BALPA – British Airline Pilots Association

SEP – Single Engine Piston

MEP – Multi Engine Piston

MCC – Multi Crew Cooperation

MPL – Multi Crew Pilot Licence

TRTO – Type Rating Training Organisation

AOC – Air Operator Certificate

AME – Authorised Medical Examiner

SO – Second Officer

FO- First Officer

SFO – Senior First Officer

Capt - Captain

TT – Total Time

FNPT – Flight and Navigation Procedures Trainer

PIC – Pilot in Command

SOP – Standard Operating Procedures

LST – Licensing Skills Test

PF – Pilot Flying

PNF – Pilot Not Flying

FFS – Full Flight Simulator

FTD – Flight Training Device

FTO – Flight Training Organisation

ATO – Approved Training Organisation

DOW – Dry Operating Weight

ATC – Air Traffic Control

OFP – Operational Flight Plan

STD – Standard Time of Departure

NOTAM – Notice To Airmen

NOTAC – Notice To Air crew

TRI – Type Rating Instructor

TRE – Type Rating Examiner

SID – Standard Instrument Departure

STAR – Standard Arrival

APPENDIX

SAMPLE JAA/EASA ATPL GROUND EXAM QUESTIONS

As already mentioned the ATPL ground school consists of 14 written exams, which are Multi Choice Style Exams. The Subjects are:

1. Human Performance and Limitations
2. Air Law and ATC Procedures,
3. Operational Procedures,
4. VFR Communications,
5. IFR Communications,
6. Meteorology,
7. Principles of Flight,
8. Performance,
9. Flight Planning,
10. General Navigation,
11. Mass and Balance,
12. Aircraft General Knowledge,
13. Instrumentation,
14. Radio Navigation

I have added a few sample questions below just to give you a brief idea of the type of questions you will see in the exams.

As you will appreciate it's not rocket science, but there is a lot of information that you will have to learn and remember, its all interesting stuff though. As I said Bristol Ground School are very good at teaching this stuff. Oxford is too.

ATPL Style Questions

PRINCIPLES OF FLIGHT

When a pilot makes a turn in horizontal flight, the stall speed:

    A increases with flap extension

    B increases with the load factor squared

    C decreases with increasing bank angle

    (D) increases with the square root of the load factor

The stalling speed is determined by:

    A the CL for maximum L/D ration

    (B) the maximum value of CL

    C the CL for zero lift

    D the CL at zero angle of attack

What action must the pilot take to maintain altitude and airspeed during a turn in a jet aircraft?

    A decrease the turn radius

    B increase the angle of attack

    C increase the thrust

    (D) increase the angle of attack and thrust

AIRCRAFT GENERAL KNOWLEDGE – SYSTEMS

An engine pressure ratio (EPR) gauge reading normally shows the ratio of:

(A) jet pipe pressure to compressor inlet pressure

B jet pipe pressure to combustion chamber pressure

C combustion chamber pressure to compressor inlet pressure

D compressor outlet pressure to compressor inlet pressure

The purposes of the oil and the nitrogen in an oleo-pneumatic strut are:

A the oil supplies the spring function and the nitrogen supplies the damping function

B the oil supplies the sealing and lubrication function, the nitrogen supplies the damping function

C the oil supplies the damping and lubrication function, the nitrogen supplies the heat-dissipation function

(D) the oil supplies the damping function and the nitrogen supplies the spring function

A unit that converts electrical DC into AC is:

A a thermistor

(B) an inverter

C an AC generator

D a transformer rectifier unit

AIRCRAFT GENERAL KNOWLEDGE – INSTRUMENTATION

In the event of a conflict, the TCAS (Traffic Collision Avoidance System) will give information such as:

A turn left/turn right

B too low terrain

C glide slope

(D) climb/descent

A pilot wishes to turn right on to a northerly heading with 20° bank at a latitude of 40° North. Using a direct reading compass, in order to achieve this he must stop the turn on to an approximate heading of:

A 010°

B 330°

(C) 350°

D 030°

The main input data to the Stall Warning Annunciator System are:

1 - Mach Meter indication

2 - Angle of Attack

3 - Indicate Airspeed (IAS)

4 - Aircraft configuration (Flaps/Slats)

The combination regrouping all the correct statements is:

A 2,3

B 1,4

C 1,2

(D) 2,4

HUMAN PERFORMANCE

An upward sloped runway can give a pilot the illusion of:

    A you are too far from the runway

    (B) you are too high

    C you are too low

    D you are too close

If a pilot were to fly whilst suffering from a cold, he/she could be affected by:

    A the chokes

    B the bends

    C blurred vision

    (D) sinus pain

Good decision making is best described as:

    A an automatic process

    B both conscious and voluntary process after assessing options

    C an arbitrary process

    (D) a systematic and analytical process

METEOROLOGY

FEW is defined as:

A   0-1 Oktas of cloud cover

(B) 1-2 Oktas of cloud cover

C   2-3 Oktas of cloud cover

D   3-4 Oktas of cloud cover

The pressure of the atmosphere:

A   decreases at an increasing rate as height increases

B   decreases at a constant rate as height increases

(C) decreases at a decreasing rate as height increases

D   decreases at a constant rate up to the tropopause and remains constant

The start of the mature stage of thunderstorm development is indicated by:

A   start of up currents

B   start of turbulence

(C) start of precipitation

D   end of up currents

AIRCRAFT PERFORMANCE

When density increases, the landing distance required will:

   A increase

   (B) decrease

   C remain the same

   D decreases then increases

When operating at the tyre limited MTOW, the maximum tyre speed will be equal to:

   A lift-off TAS

   B lift-off EAS

   C lift-off IAS

   (D) lift off groundspeed

The speed range between low and high speed buffet:

   A decreases with increasing mass and is independent of altitude

   (B) narrows with increasing mass and increasing altitude

   C is only limiting at low altitudes

   D increases with increasing mass

IFR COMMUNICATIONS

What does the abbreviation "IMC" mean?

(A) instrument meteorological conditions

B International meteorological channel

C in most cases

D international meteorological conditions

What is the correct way of transmitting the phrases, 118.1?

A eight one

B one one eight point one

C eight decimal one

(D) one one eight decimal one

What does the term "Expected Approach Time" mean?

A The holding time over the radio facility from which the instrument approach procedure for landing will be initiated

(B) The time at which ATC expects that an arriving aircraft, following a delay, will leave the holding point to complete its approach for a landing

C The time at which an arriving aircraft, upon reaching the radio aid serving the destination aerodrome, will commence the instrument approach procedure for a landing

D The time at which an arriving aircraft expects to arrive over the appropriate designated navigation aid serving the destination aerodrome

VFR COMMUNICATIONS

What does the phrase "go ahead" mean:

   A Yes

   B Pass me the following information

   (C) Proceed with you message

   D Taxi on

Which abbreviation is used for the term "control zone"?

   A CTA

   B CTZ

   (C) CTR

   D CZ

A message concerning an aircraft being threatened by grave and imminent danger, requiring immediate assistance is called:

   A Urgency message

   (B) Distress message

   C Flight safety message

   D Class B message

GENERAL NAVIGATION

The ICAO definition of ETA is the:

(A) estimated time of arrival at destination

B actual time of arrival at a point or fix

C estimated time of arrival at an en-route point or fix

D estimated time en route

Given: GS = 480 kt.
Distance from A to B = 5360 NM.
What is the time from A to B?

A 11 HR 15 MIN

(B) 11 HR 10 MIN

C 11 HR 06 MIN

D 11 HR 07 MIN

An aircraft is planned to fly from position 'A' to position 'B',distance 320 NM, at an average GS of 180 kt. It departs 'A' at 1200 UTC. After flying 70 NM along track from 'A', the aircraft is 3 MIN ahead of planned time. Using the actual GS experienced, what is the revised ETA at 'B'?

(A) 1333 UTC

B 1401 UTC

C 1347 UTC

D 1340 UTC

RADIO NAVIGATION

What airborne equipment, if any, is required to be fitted in order that a VDF let-down may be flown?

A VOR/DME

(B) VHF radio

C VOR

D none

Under JAR-25 colour code rules, features displayed in green on an Electronic Flight Instrument System (EFIS), indicate:

(A) engaged modes

B cautions, abnormal sources

C the earth

D the ILS deviation pointer

An NDB transmits a signal pattern in the horizontal plane which is:

(A) omnidirectional

B bi-lobal circular

C a cardioid balanced at 30 Hz

D a beam rotating at 30 Hz

FLIGHT PLANNING

In an ATS flight plan, Item 15 (route), a cruising pressure altitude of 32000 feet would be entered as:

(A) FL320

B S3200

C 32000

D F320

From which of the following would you expect to find facilitation information (FAL) regarding customs and health formalities?

(A) AIP (Air Information Publication)

B NAV/RAD charts

C ATCC

D NOTAM

From which of the following would you expect to find information regarding known short unserviceability of VOR, TACAN, and NDB?

(A) NOTAM

B AIP (Air Information Publication)

C SIGMET

D ATCC broadcasts

MASS & BALANCE

The actual 'Zero Fuel Mass' is equal to the:

    A Basic Empty Mass plus the fuel loaded

    B Actual Landing Mass plus trip fuel

    C Dry Operating Mass plus the traffic load

    (D) Operating Mass plus all the traffic load

With the centre of gravity on the forward limit which of the following is to be expected?

    A A decrease in the landing speed

    B A decrease of the stalling speed

    C A tendency to yaw to the right on take-off

    (D) A decrease in range

The term 'useful load' as applied to an aeroplane includes:

    A the revenue-earning portion of traffic load only

    B the revenue-earning portion of traffic load plus useable fuel

    (C) traffic load plus useable fuel

    D traffic load only

OPERATIONAL PROCEDURES

The authorization for the transport of hazardous materials is specified on the:

   A insurance certificate

   (B) air carrier certificate

   C registration certificate

   D airworthiness certificate

The captain is asked by the authority to present the documents of the aircraft. He:

   A can refuse to present them

   B can only do so after having consulted the operator

   (C) must do so, within a reasonable period of time

   D can request a delay of 48 hours

Flight crew members on the flight deck shall keep their safety belt fastened:

   A from take off to landing

   (B) while at their station

   C only during take off and landing

   D only during take off and landing and whenever necessary by the commander in the interest of safety

AIR LAW

The age of an applicant for a commercial pilot licence shall not be less than:

(A) 17 years of age

B 16 years of age

C 18 years of age

D 21 years of age

The speed limitation for IFR flights inside ATS airspace classified as C, when flying below 3.050 m (10.000 ft) AMSL, is:

A Not applicable

B 250 KT IAS

(C) 250 KT TAS

D 240 KT IAS

Which code shall be used on Mode "A" to provide recognition of an aircraft subjected to unlawful interference?

A Code 7600

B Code 2000

(C) Code 7500

D Code 7700

Website List

www.caa.co.uk

www.balpa.org

www.stormmcginley.com

www.ontrackaviation.com

www.caa.co.uk/aocholders

www.flightglobal.com

www.pilotjobsnetwork.com

www.coffeelovesmilk.com

www.ipapilot.com

www.bristol.gs

www.oaa.com

www.airwaysflighttraining.co.uk

www.bristol-aviation.co.uk

www.flyaft.com

www.propilot.eu/your-career/west-atlantic-cadet-scheme

www.bafuturepilot.com

www.ctcwings.co.uk

www.ftejerez.com

www.flyingscholarship.co.uk

www.gapan.org/career-matters/scholarships/

www.rafa.org.uk/images/library/files/Flying_Scholarship_Application_Form_2010.pdf

www.airleague.co.uk/scholarships/

www.pprune.com

www.oddsoft.co.uk/rant2000.html

www.brookfieldav.com

how2become

Visit www.how2become.co.uk to find more titles and courses that will help you to pass any selection process or interview.

- Online psychometric testing
- 1-day training courses
- Career guidance books and DVD's
- Psychometric testing books and CDs.

www.how2become.co.uk